ELVIS

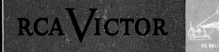

ELVIS

RCA VICTOR
A ''New Orthophonic'' High Fidelity Record

ELVIS THE ULTIMATE ALBUM COVER BOOK

BY PAUL DOWLING

HARRY N. ABRAMS, INC., PUBLISHERS

This book is dedicated to my mother, who
passed away in 1989. She was always
there for me, no matter what.

Editor: Elisa Urbanelli
Designer: Ellen Nygaard Ford
All photographs by Gabe Palacio

Library of Congress Cataloging-in-
Publication Data

Dowling, Paul, 1945–
    Elvis, the ultimate album cover book /
  by Paul Dowling.
      p. cm.
    ISBN 0-8109-3268-7 (hard cover)
    1. Presley, Elvis, 1935-1977—
    Discographies. 2. Sound recordings—
Album covers. I. Title.
ML156.7.P7D69   1996
782.42166'092—dc20   96-1708

Published in 1996 by Harry N. Abrams,
Incorporated, New York
A Times Mirror Company

Printed and bound in Hong Kong

CONTENTS

FOLLOW THAT DREAM

I was born in 1945. When Elvis Presley first achieved fame in 1956, I was ten years old and not at all interested in popular music. Two years later rock 'n' roll eventually entered my life—but not by way of Elvis. I was busy buying records by Fabian and Frankie Avalon. The only thing I knew about Elvis was that he was in the army! One day in 1962 I went to see the movie *Follow That Dream*. By then I had heard Elvis's music and seen his face in photographs, but that afternoon was the first time I had ever witnessed him in action. As I watched Elvis on the screen playing a dumb but likable hillbilly, something clicked. It is difficult to say what it was about Elvis that grabbed me, but whatever it was, it would never go away. I didn't go out immediately and buy Elvis's records. I waited until 1964 when a local Baltimore radio station had a one-hour Elvis program every night. I taped all of the shows on a reel-to-reel tape recorder. After listening to the tapes over and over again, I realized how much I loved his songs and his voice. I began buying a single here, an LP there, but never considered collecting records seriously. My main concern, at that time, was just to hear everything that he had recorded. I couldn't get enough of his music. In 1969 I read an article in *Elvis Monthly*, an English magazine that is still in print, about Elvis records from foreign countries and how their covers varied from those of the U.S. releases. It had never occurred to me that other countries put out anything different from the records I was used to seeing here in stores. Once I read this, I was hooked on the idea of owning Elvis records from around the world. The only problem was that I had no notion of where to go or whom to contact in order to find these long-out-of-print records. What would be the likelihood of locating people with access to old releases from the 1950s and 1960s, especially in far-flung countries such as South Africa, Japan, and Australia? In late 1972 I came across a notice for *Elvis Weekly*, a publication (also from England) that contained names and addresses of collectors in many countries. At last, I found what I had been looking for. I wrote to anyone and everyone, asking my new pen pals to send lists of records from their countries that were different from the U.S. releases. I'll never forget that day in March 1973 when my sea mail order from Haruo Hirose in Japan arrived with the *Elvis' Golden Story Vols. 1 and 2, Golden Hymns,* and *Girl Happy* LPs. Little did I know how that first package would change my life. From that point on I pledged that I wouldn't rest until I obtained every foreign record I possibly could. Thus began my perpetual worldwide search for Elvis records. Once I began corresponding with serious Elvis collectors like myself in more than forty countries, I discovered that so much had been—and was still being—released. Getting it all would be an endless, but gratifying, task. It was an addiction! The only thing I really cared about was getting more and more records. And the more records I accumulated, it seemed the more I needed. Soon it became apparent that collecting all the Elvis records in the world would not be a cheap hobby. I had borrowed money from my parents, my sister, and my friends and spent every cent on records. I needed to find a way to support my "Elvis habit," so I started selling extra copies of records I already had in order to buy new additions to my personal collection. Before long, I had turned a hobby into a business. In 1974 (three years before Elvis died) I formed a company to sell original Elvis records to collectors all over the world. Twenty-two years later, running Worldwide Elvis remains my full-time occupation. Thanks to all of my international pen pals, I have more than seven thousand different Elvis 78s, singles, EPs, and LPs from more than sixty countries. Believe it or not, I'm still looking for items I don't have. I first had the idea for this book seventeen years ago. Finally, it has become a reality. I hope you enjoy looking at these wonderful and surprising record covers, some of which have rarely been seen—even by many serious Elvis collectors.

Paul Dowling, 1996

KING OF THE WHOLE WIDE WORLD

There has never been anyone like Elvis Presley in the history of recorded music. A bold statement, but one that is difficult to dispute. First of all, he has sold more records internationally than any other artist. His likeness is as recognizable around the world as Mickey Mouse or Coca-Cola. And, simply put, he changed the course of popular music. Although he hardly invented the genre, Elvis is known as "The King of Rock 'n' Roll." By blending gospel, rhythm and blues, and country music he created a style that was undeniably his own. No one could mistake that voice, whether it was singing soulful blues, rockabilly, hymns, or romantic ballads. No one could mistake that "look" either. With his slicked-back hair and flamboyant clothes, the young Elvis looked like a juvenile delinquent, an unseemly character who horrified parents and drove teenagers wild. His stage movements—the snarl, the shaky legs, the gyrating hips—conveyed a raw sensuality that had never been given such public display in mainstream white America. Offstage, Elvis portrayed a different side: somewhat shy, religious, very polite, and family oriented. The combination of talent, looks, and a good guy/bad guy persona assured his stardom. In April 1953, Elvis Presley walked into the Memphis Recording Service building (owned by Sam Phillips) in Memphis, Tennessee, and recorded two songs: "My Happiness" and "That's When Your Heartaches Begin." A little over a year later, in July 1954, he began his professional career with "That's All Right" for Phillips's Sun Records. Elvis was with the Sun label for only sixteen months, releasing a total of five singles, but in that short period of time he launched a new era in popular music. His first singles, not to mention his performances, created such a stir in the South that by November 1955 Elvis had attracted a persuasive manager, the legendary Colonel Tom Parker, and had captured the attention of RCA Records, which bought Elvis's contract from Sun for $40,000. When Elvis mania hit the United States in early 1956, it would not be long before RCA began promoting the star throughout the world. Since then, his records have been pressed and issued in Argentina, Australia, Austria, Belgium, Bolivia, Brazil, Canada, Chile, China, Colombia, Cuba, Denmark, England, Finland, France, Germany, Greece, Holland, Hong Kong, Iceland, India, Ireland, Israel, Italy, Japan, Korea, Lebanon, Mexico, New Zealand, Norway, Peru, Portugal, South Africa, Spain, Sweden, Switzerland, Turkey, Uruguay, Venezuela, the former Yugoslavia, and more than twenty other countries. It took some countries longer than others to release Elvis records, but once they did there was no turning back. With the exception of a few soundtrack songs, Elvis never recorded in any language other than English. However, the titles of his songs were often translated on the covers of his foreign records. In most countries his records were released with A and B sides that varied from the corresponding U.S. releases. Why? In order to sell as many records to as many fans as possible, RCA and its licensees in each country had to determine if the collection of songs, as it was compiled for the American audience, would appeal to fans in their country or if a specific compilation geared to those fans would sell more copies. Changing the compilation meant, for example, that instead of releasing "Don't Be Cruel" as the flip side of "Hound Dog," "Guadalajara" was chosen in an attempt to appeal to Mexican fans. This scheme took advantage of the local popularity of certain Elvis songs that might never have been singles in the United States. Likewise, EPs and LPs were issued in foreign markets with songs never compiled in the same format in this country. It might not seem like an economical approach to making records, but customizing collections of songs that were hits in other countries proved to be a smart strategy for catering to an international audience. Elvis was first introduced to foreign fans through his record releases, and this meant not only through the music itself, but also through how it was packaged. Record covers were integral to the phenomenon of marketing Elvis to the world. RCA found that changing covers from country to country could dramatically increase sales. Every affiliate of the company used this formula and, at one time or another, released an Elvis 78, single, EP, or LP unique to that country. Sometimes the original U.S. cover design was used but merely translated into a different language; other times the cover was given an alternate background color, type style, or graphic treatment. Still other covers bore no resemblance to the corresponding U.S. releases. The cover photographs were sometimes manipulated slightly to make Elvis appear, for example, Asian or Latin. Of course, the production of so many variations has created some very collectible items in the process. Although the records pictured in this book constitute a small number of the total released, this sampling gives one a good idea of how RCA's affiliates presented the image of Elvis around the globe. Also evident in these pages is how Elvis himself evolved over the years—from his early Memphis years as a rock 'n' roller, to his meteoric rise as an international star, to his fun-loving movie roles of the 1960s, to his sensational Las Vegas comeback. Revealed is the phenomenal scope of Elvis's popularity. No other artist's record catalogue has come close to equaling his in size and international range. He not only conquered the United States, but along the way became "King of the Whole Wide World."

ABOUT THE CAPTIONS

The caption for each record cover contains the following information: title; country of origin; notation of format (78, single, EP [extended play], 10" LP [long-playing], or 12" LP); and date of release (year and, if available, month and day that the record was issued).

EPs were small LPs. They were the same seven-inch size as a single and were normally played at the same 45 RPM (revolutions per minute) speed, but they generally included two songs per side. The standard size of an LP was twelve inches in diameter, but some countries (for example, Chile, England, France, Italy, Japan, and South Africa) released smaller ten-inch LPs that played at the standard 33⅓ RPM LP speed.

The covers are organized by decade and grouped by release so one can see how different countries packaged the same or related compilations. Later versions of releases are included with earlier ones; therefore covers in the 1950s category, for example, may be shown alongside related covers from the later decades.

195s

Sun Records

The five singles Elvis recorded on the Sun label were released in both 45 RPM and 78 RPM formats and came in the now famous "sunburst" sleeves. RCA first reissued the singles in plain sleeves in November 1955. The songs were subsequently rereleased in the United States and other countries with picture covers.

SUN SINGLES

Top left: **That's All Right / Blue Moon of Kentucky**
July 19, 1954

Top right: **Good Rockin' Tonight / I Don't Care If the Sun Don't Shine**
September 25, 1954

Center: **Milkcow Blues Boogie / You're a Heartbreaker**
January 8, 1955

Bottom left: **Baby Let's Play House / I'm Left, You're Right, She's Gone**
April 30, 1955

Bottom right: **Mystery Train / I Forgot to Remember to Forget**
August 6, 1955

Good Rockin' Tonight

"Good Rockin' Tonight"
England (EP)
September 1957

Photo: 20th Century-Fox

"Good Rockin' Tonight"

* BLUE MOON OF KENTUCKY

     * GOOD ROCKIN' TONIGHT

* MILK COW BLUES

* JUST BECAUSE

ELVIS PRESLEY

"HIS MASTER'S VOICE"
EXTENDED PLAY 45 r.p.m. RECORD

14

GOOD ROCKIN' TONIGHT

Good rockin' tonight
I don't care if the sun don't shine
That's all right
Blue moon of Kentucky
Baby let's play house
I'm left, you're right, she's gone
Milkcow blues boogie
You're a heartbreaker

ELVIS

PRESLEY

RCA

130.252

**Good Rockin'
Tonight**
France (10" LP)
1957

15

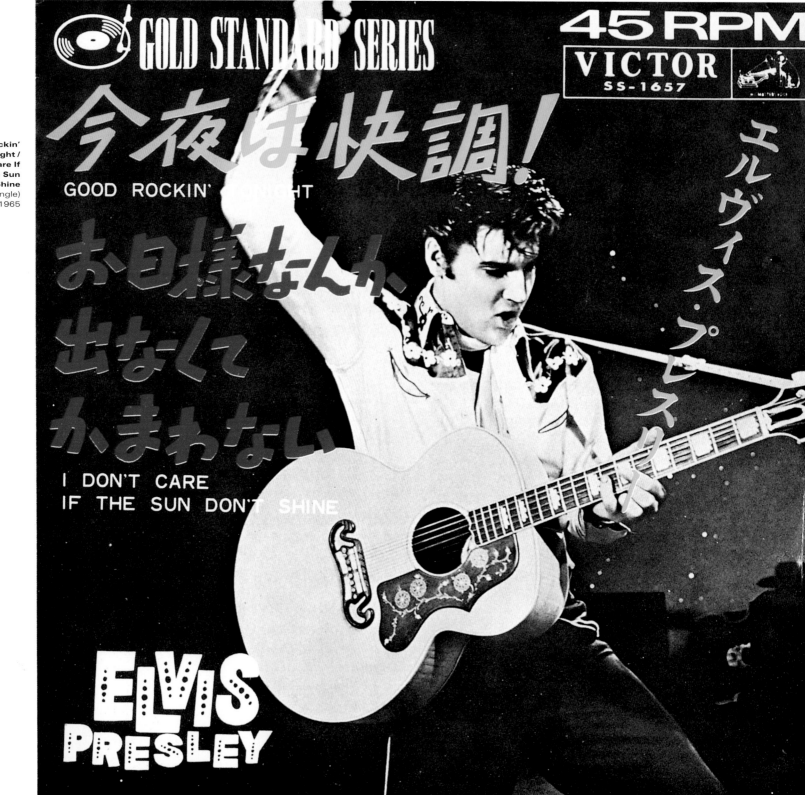

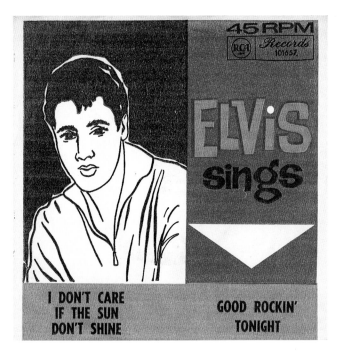

**Elvis Sings
(I Don't Care If the
Sun Don't Shine /
Good Rockin' Tonight)**
Australia (single)
May 1965

**Blue Moon /
Tryin' to Get to You**
Japan (single)
December 1958

78 RPM Covers

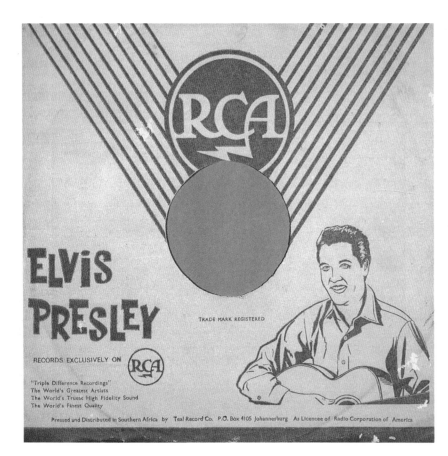

78 cover
South Africa (generic)
1961 and 1962

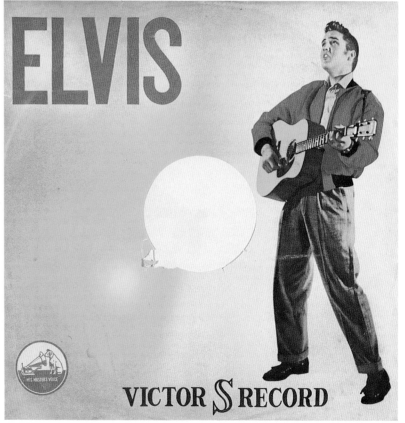

78 cover
Japan (generic)
1956

*During the 1950s and early 1960s, 78- and
45-RPM–speed records were issued simultaneously
in most countries. The 78s often came in generic
sleeves.*

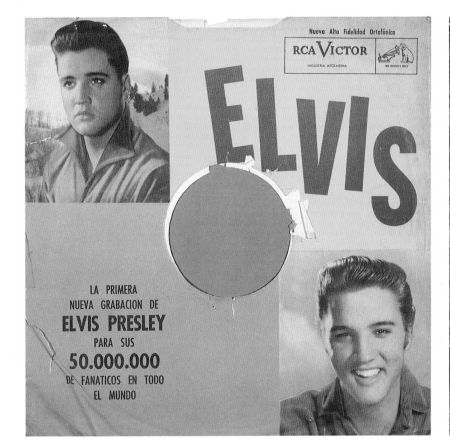

Stuck On You /
Fame and Fortune
Argentina (78 RPM)
1960

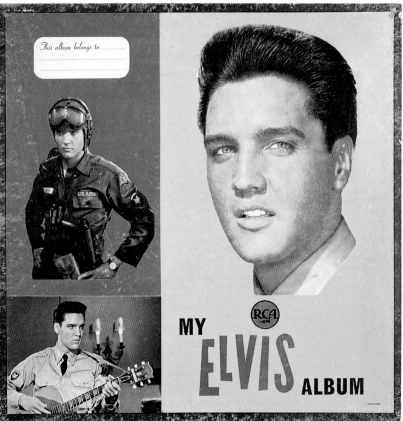

My Elvis Album
South Africa (LP storage box)
1961

This unusual item is not an album
at all, but rather a storage box
that holds up to seven LPs.

The First LP

Titled simply Elvis Presley, *Elvis's first LP appeared in March 1956 (opposite). With its bold pink-and-green lettering, the cover is one of the most widely recognized—and imitated—in the history of rock 'n' roll. The design was adapted by RCA affiliates in many countries for various Elvis compilations.*

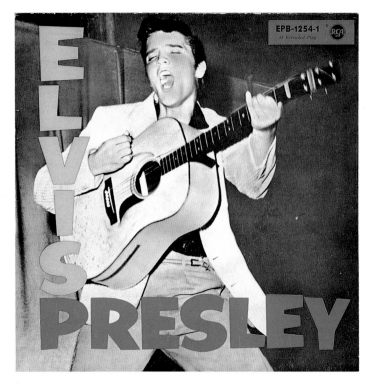

Elvis Presley
Germany (EP)
1956

Rock and Roll
Spain (LP)
1959

Elvis Presley
United States (LP)
March 23, 1956

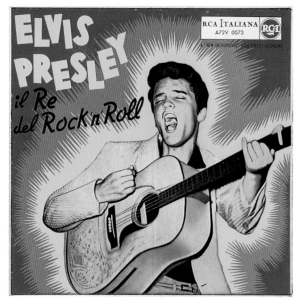

Il Re del Rock 'n' Roll
Italy (EP)
December 1956

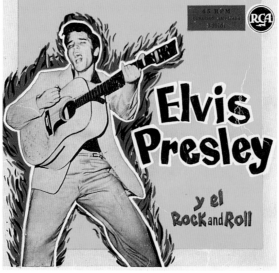

Y el Rock and Roll
Spain (EP)
1958

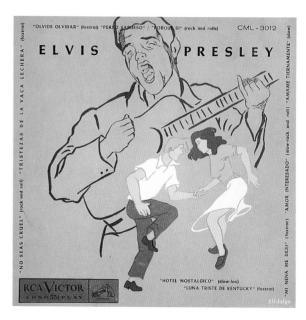

Elvis Presley
Chile (10" LP)
January 1957

ELVIS

LA PELVIS

RCA VICTOR
A ''New Orthophonic'' High Fidelity Recording

Elvis la Pelvis
Argentina (LP)
May 1988

Elvis and Others

Elvis was introduced to audiences in some countries by being featured in collections of songs with other established RCA artists. In South Africa, for example, RCA issued a ten-inch LP with four songs by Elvis—all Sun recordings—and four songs by Janis Martin, a rockabilly singer from Virginia who was billed as "the female Elvis." Her claim to fame was a single called "My Boy Elvis."

Janis and Elvis
South Africa (10" LP)
1957

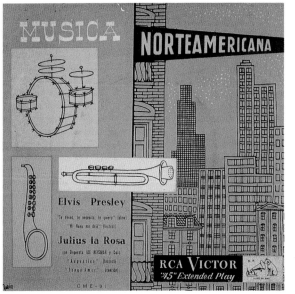

Musica Norteamericana
Chile (EP)
December 1956

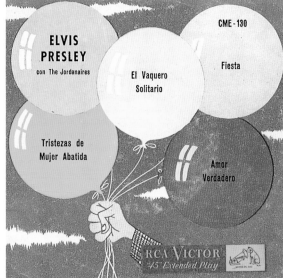

Elvis Presley
Chile (EP)
1957

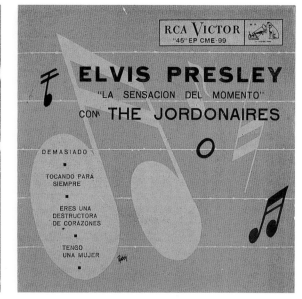

La Sensacion del Momento
Chile (EP)
1956

*Early in Elvis's career, covers with photographs of the
rising star were not considered essential selling tools,
as these three EPs from Chile demonstrate. The EP on
the left paired Elvis with a popular singer named
Julius la Rosa.*

Cocktail di successi N. 5
Italy (10″ LP)
September 1957

RCA ITALIANA
A10V 0109

RCA

A "NEW ORTHOPHONIC" HIGH FIDELITY RECORDING

COCKTAIL DI SUCCESSI N. 5

EARTHA KITT
- JUST AN OLD FASHIONED GIRL
- LISBOA ANTIGUA

ELVIS PRESLEY
- ALL SHOOK UP
- LOVING YOU

HARRY BELAFONTE
- BANANA BOAT
- SCARLET RIBBONS

DINAH SHORE
- I'LL COME BACK
- PROMISES, PROMISES

PERRY COMO
- ROUND AND ROUND
- THE GIRL WITH THE GOLDEN BRAIDS

HARRY BELAFONTE : ISLAND IN THE SUN · SOPHIA LOREN : S'AGAPO · ELVIS PRESLEY : GOT A LOT O' LIVIN' TO DO!
DEBBIE REYNOLDS · EDDIE FISHER : LULLABY IN BLUE · MARIO LANZA : BECAUSE YOU'RE MINE · THE AMES BROTHERS : TAMMY
MARILYN MONROE : AFTER YOU GET WHAT YOU WANT · JULIUS LA ROSA : MAMA GUITAR · DINAH SHORE : FASCINATION
PERRY COMO : SOMEBODY UP THERE LIKES ME · LENA HORNE : STORMY WEATHER · ELIO MAURO : LLARI-LLIRA

RCA ITALIANA
LPM 10003
A "New Orthophonic" High Fidelity Recording

Cocktail
di successi
N. 8
SELEZIONI DA FILMS

**Cocktail di
successi N. 8**
Italy (LP)
December 1957

*A group of "cock-
tail" LPs from Italy
mixed Elvis with
such performers as
Eartha Kitt, Harry
Belafonte, Dinah
Shore, Perry Como,
Lena Horne, and
Sophia Loren.*

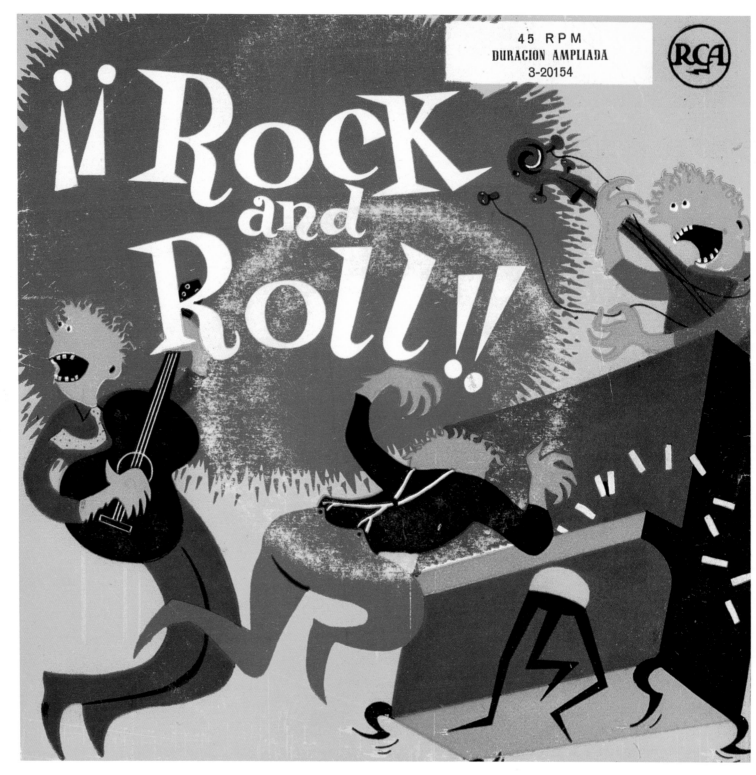

¡¡Rock and Roll!!
Spain (EP)
1958

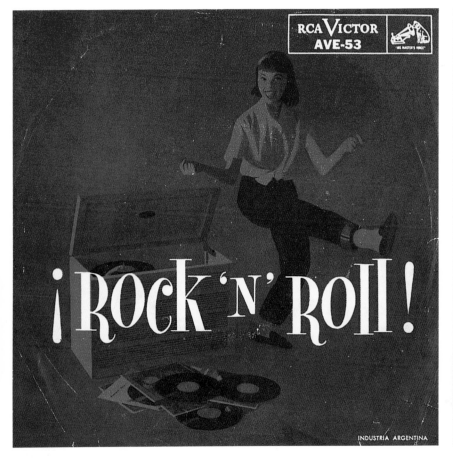

¡Rock 'n' Roll!
Argentina (EP)
April 1958

Rock and Roll
Chile (EP)
June 1956

The Real Elvis

This group of covers features Elvis performing on one of the early Dorsey Brothers TV shows. Photographs from the same show served as the basis for the design of a number of foreign releases.

Elvis Presley
Chile (10" LP)
July 1956

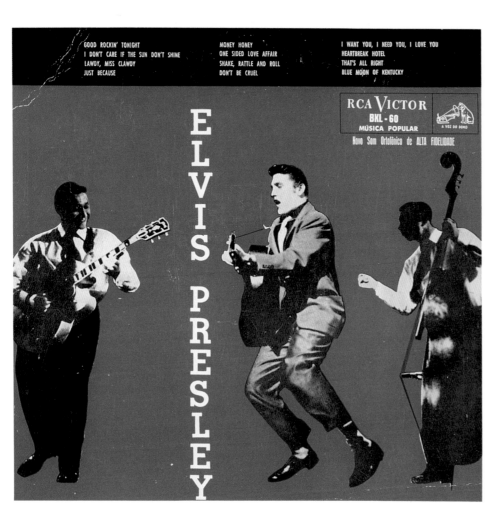

Elvis Presley
Brazil (LP)
1956

Don't Be Cruel • Hound Dog • My Baby Left Me
I Want You, I Need You, I Love You

EPA-940

The
Real
Elvis

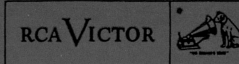
RCA VICTOR
A "NEW ORTHOPHONIC" HIGH FIDELITY RECORDING

Elvis
Presley

© RCA Printed in U. S. A.

The Real Elvis
United States (EP)
August 17, 1956

El ritmo de Elvis Presley
Spain (EP)
1962

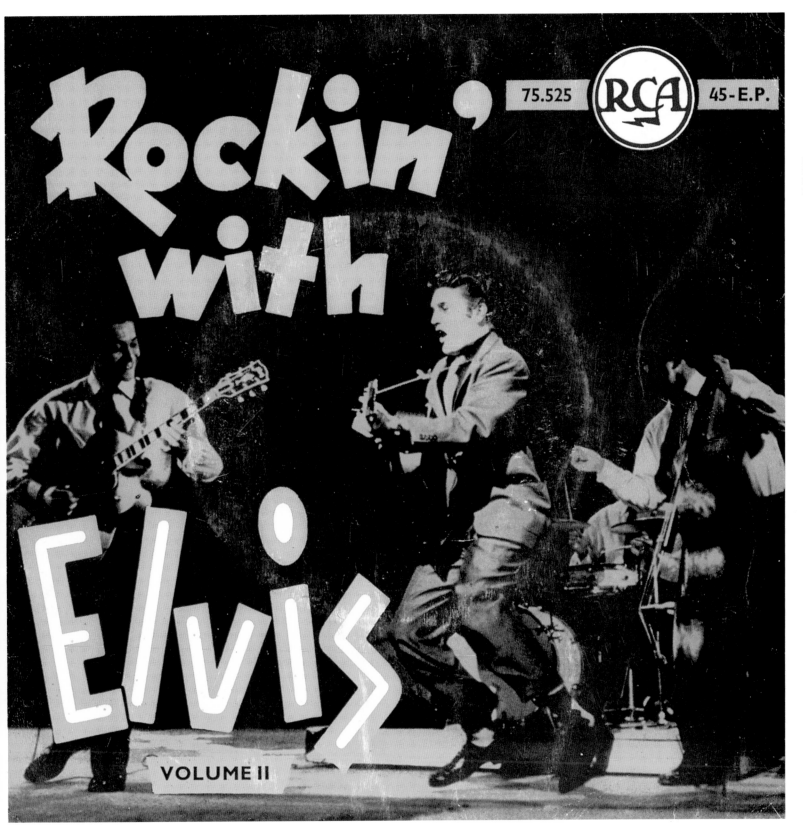

Rockin' with
Elvis Vol. II
Belgium (EP)
December 1956

Hound Dog

"Hound Dog" was Elvis's first U.S. single to be issued with a picture cover. The photograph, taken during rehearsals for the Steve Allen TV show, captured Elvis in action with his back to the camera. RCA Italiana used a photograph from the same session for its cover of Rock 'n' Roll—it's hard to believe that the song "Hound Dog" is not on the record! One of the rarest singles from any country, the 1962 Spanish release (opposite page) features a cover photo of Elvis in his famous gold lamé jacket singing to the RCA mascot, Nipper.

**Hound Dog /
Don't Be Cruel**
United States
(single)
July 13, 1956

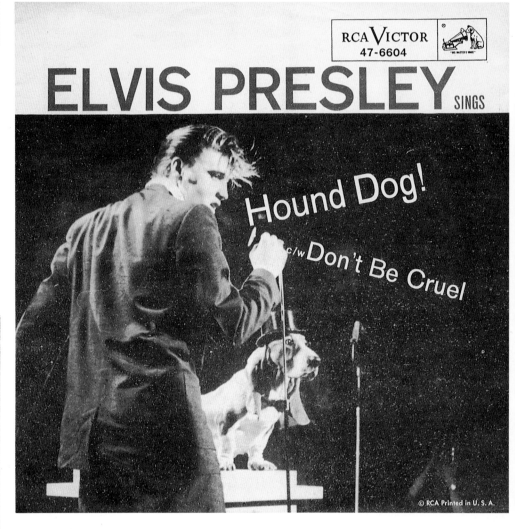

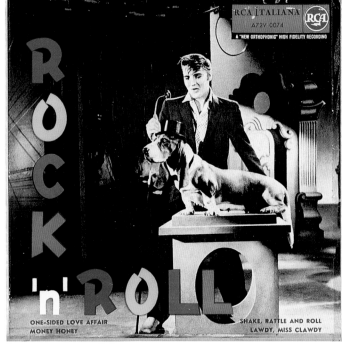

Rock 'n' Roll
Italy (EP)
December 1956

ELVIS PRESLEY

PERRO DE CAZA
NO SEAS CRUEL

**Perro de Caza /
No Seas Cruel**
Spain (single)
1962

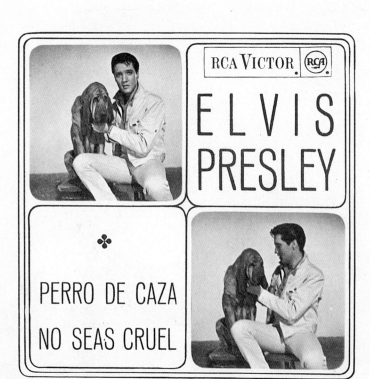

Perro de Caza / No Seas Cruel
Spain (single)
1968

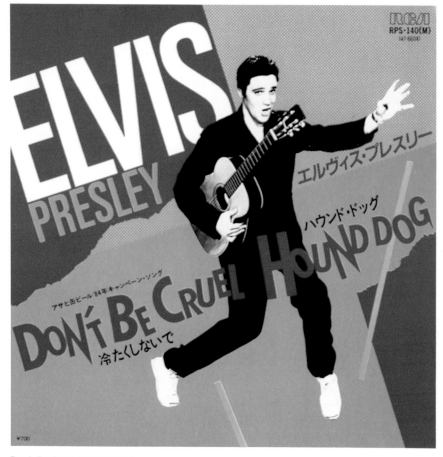

Don't Be Cruel / Hound Dog
Japan (single)
May 1984

Hound Dog /
Don't Be Cruel
Japan (single)
July 1977

Love Me Tender

**Love Me Tender /
Any Way You Want Me**
United States (single)
September 28, 1956

Love Me Tender
Japan (EP)
January 1957

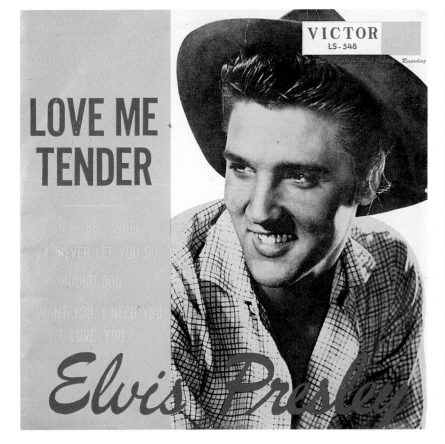

Love Me Tender
Japan (10" LP)
February 1957

Love Me Tender
England (EP)
February 1957

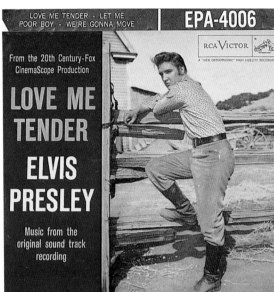

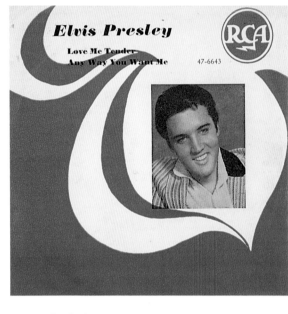

Love Me Tender
United States (EP)
November 21, 1956

**Love Me Tender /
Any Way You Want Me**
Denmark (single)
1958

Love Me Tender
Belgium (EP)
December 1956

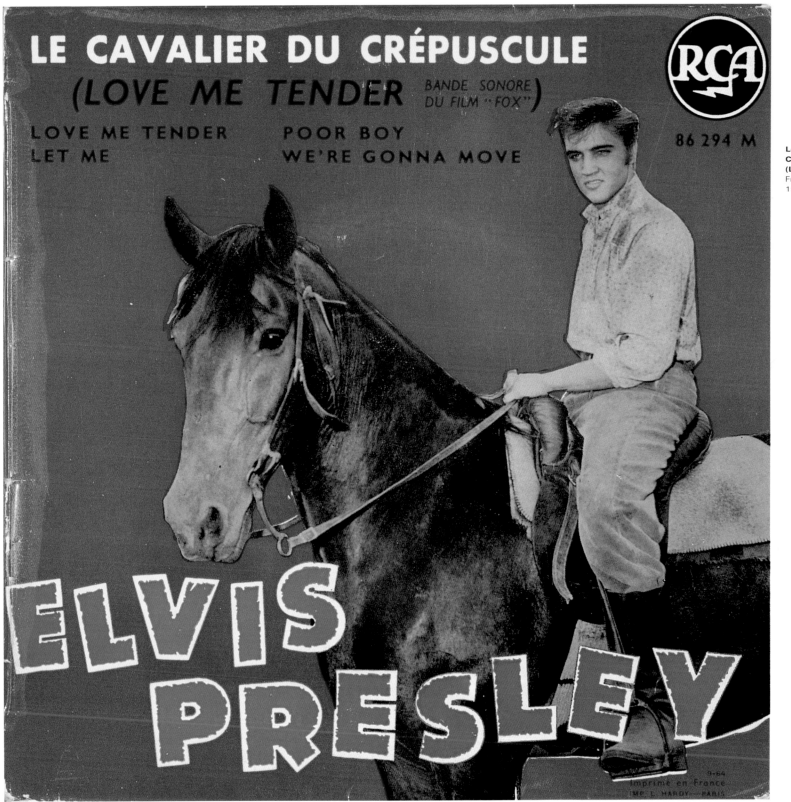

LE CAVALIER DU CRÉPUSCULE
(LOVE ME TENDER BANDE SONORE DU FILM "FOX")

LOVE ME TENDER   POOR BOY
LET ME   WE'RE GONNA MOVE

RCA

86 294 M

ELVIS PRESLEY

Le Cavalier du
Crépuscule
(Love Me Tender)
France (EP)
1961

The Second LP

Elvis
United States (LP)
October 19, 1956

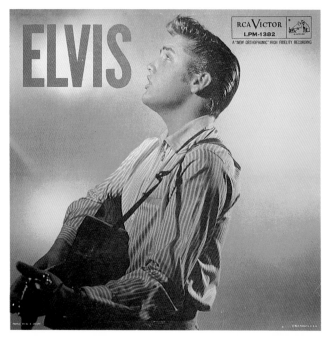

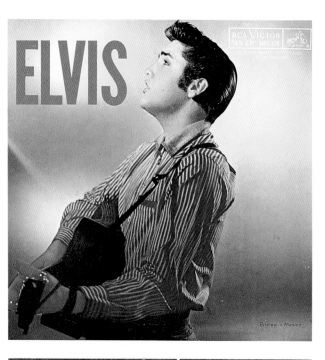

**Elvis
(Don't Be Cruel)**
Mexico (EP)
1956

**All Shook Up /
That's When Your
Heartaches Begin**
United States
(single)
March 22, 1957

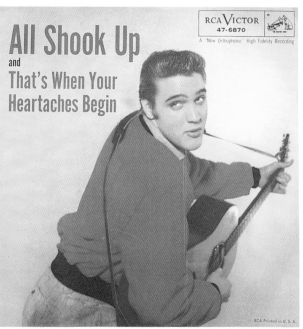

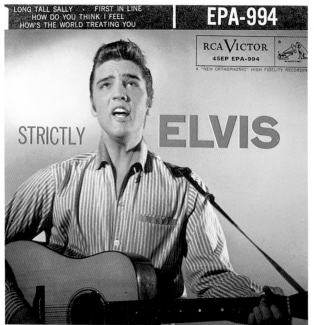

Strictly Elvis
United States (EP)
January 25, 1957

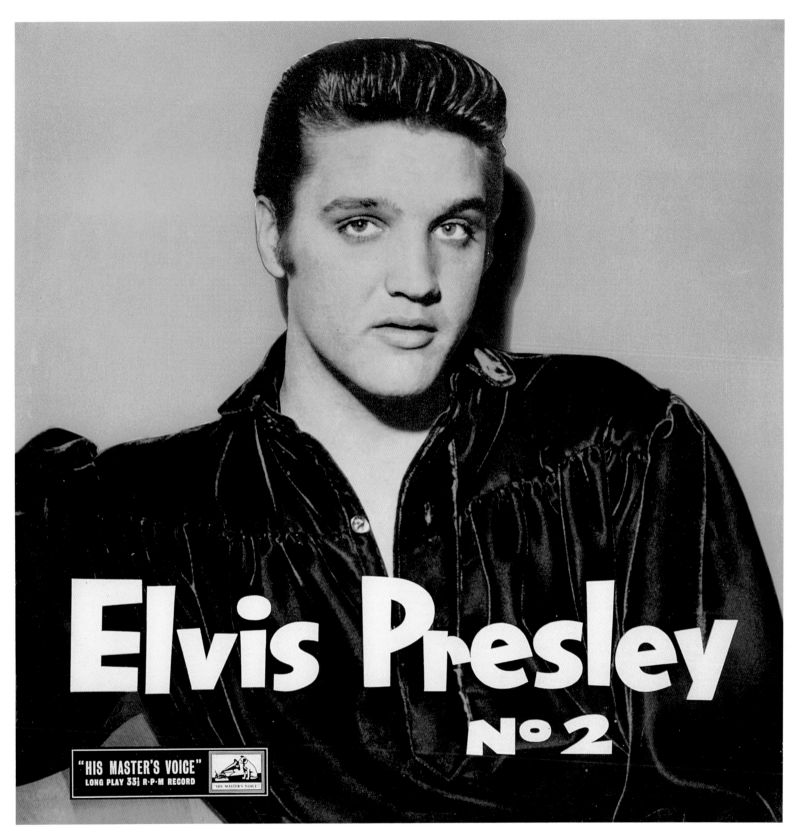

Elvis Presley
No. 2
England (LP)
April 1957

Rockin' Presley

Rockin' Presley
Denmark (EP)
1958

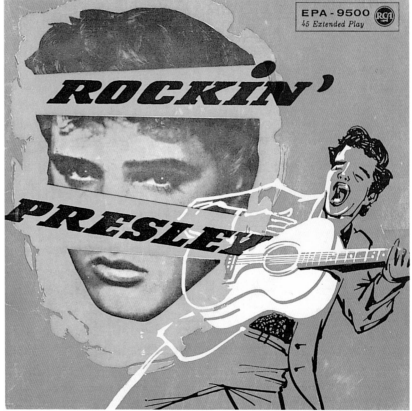

Rockin' Presley
Norway (EP)
1957

Teddy Bear

ELVIS PRESLEY

RCA VICTOR
47-7000

A "NEW ORTHOPHONIC" HIGH FIDELITY RECORDING

Teddy Bear

c/w Loving You

From Hal Wallis' Production
LOVING YOU
A Paramount Picture
in VistaVision
and Technicolor

Teddy Bear / Loving You
United States (single)
June 11, 1957

**Dejame Ser Tu Osito
de Felpa (Teddy Bear)**
Chile (EP)
1957

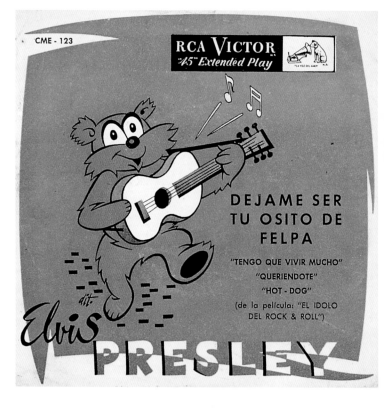

CME - 123

RCA VICTOR
"45" Extended Play

DEJAME SER
TU OSITO DE
FELPA

"TENGO QUE VIVIR MUCHO"

"QUERIENDOTE"

"HOT - DOG"

(de la película: "EL IDOLO
DEL ROCK & ROLL")

Elvis
PRESLEY

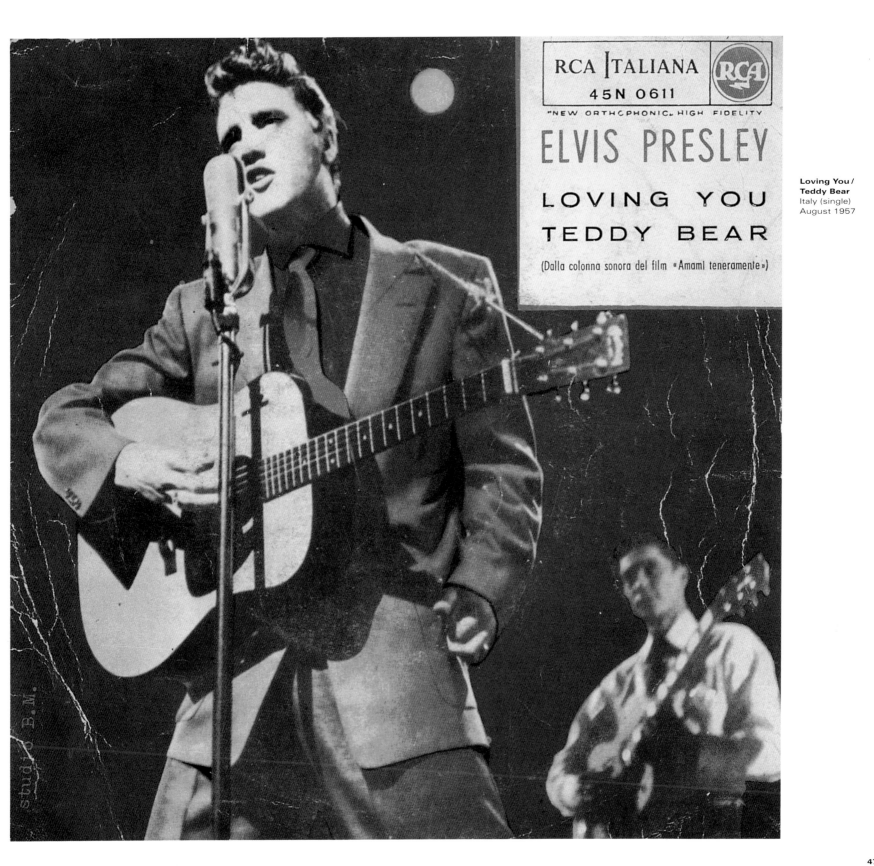

RCA ITALIANA RCA
45N 0611
"NEW ORTHOPHONIC. HIGH FIDELITY

ELVIS PRESLEY

LOVING YOU

TEDDY BEAR

(Dalla colonna sonora del film «Amami teneramente»)

**Loving You /
Teddy Bear**
Italy (single)
August 1957

studio B.M.

Loving You

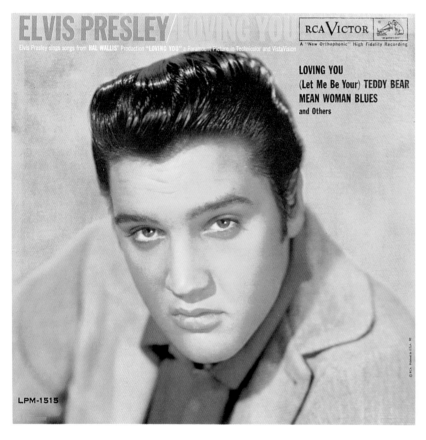

Loving You
United States (LP)
July 1, 1957

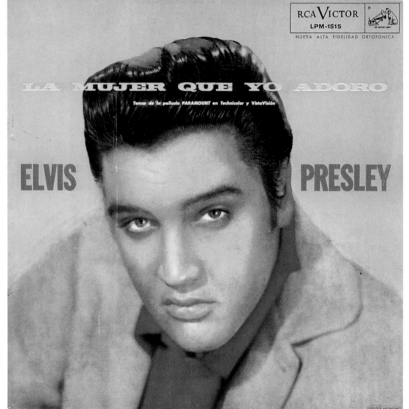

**La Mujer Que Yo
Adoro (Loving You)**
Uruguay (LP)
1957

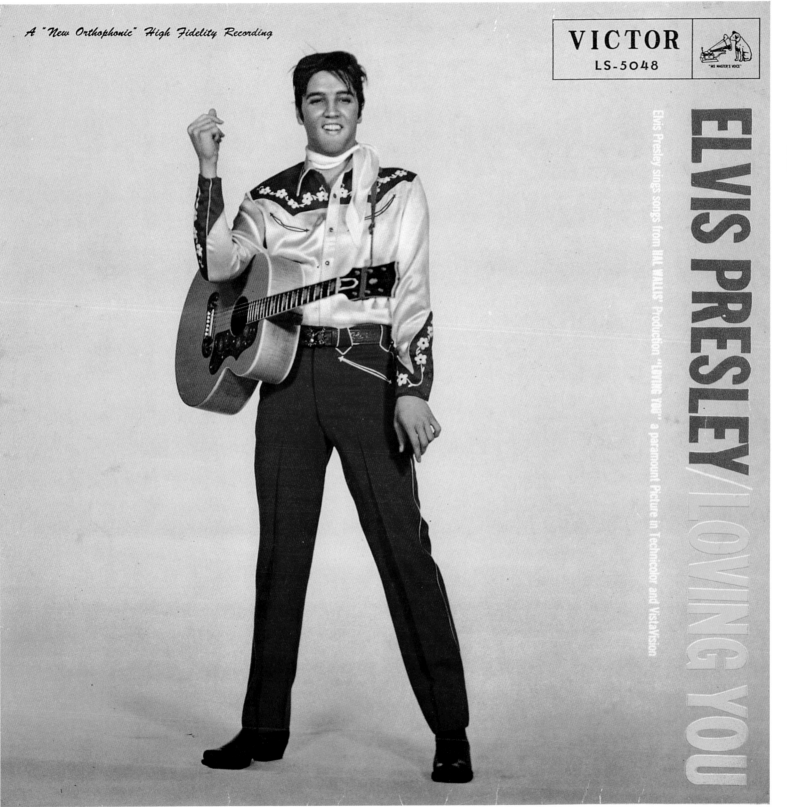

VICTOR
LS-5048

ELVIS PRESLEY/LOVING YOU

Elvis Presley sings songs from HAL WALLIS' Production "LOVING YOU" a paramount Picture in Technicolor and VistaVision

Loving You
Japan (LP)
February 1958

Jailhouse Rock /
Treat Me Nice
Mexico (single)
1977

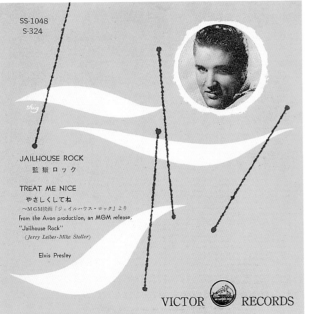

Jailhouse Rock /
Treat Me Nice
Japan (single)
November 1957

Jailhouse Rock
Japan (EP)
July 1961

Jailhouse Rock
Japan (EP)
December 1957

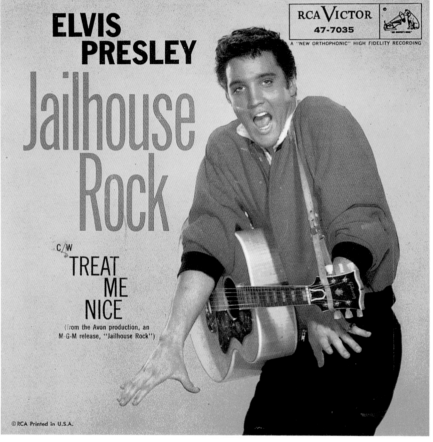

Jailhouse Rock / Treat Me Nice
United States (single)
September 24, 1957

PRESLEY GOLDEN COMPACT SERIES

SCP-1241

「監獄ロック/エルヴィス・プレスリー」

監獄ロック　　　　　　　　自由になりたい
ヤング・アンド・ビューティフル　　ドント・リーヴ・ミー・ナウ
　　　　　　　　　　　　　ベビー・アイ・ドント・ケア

VICTOR

Jailhouse Rock
Japan (EP)
December 1965

King Creole

King Creole
United States (LP)
September 19, 1958

King Creole
Mexico (EP)
1958

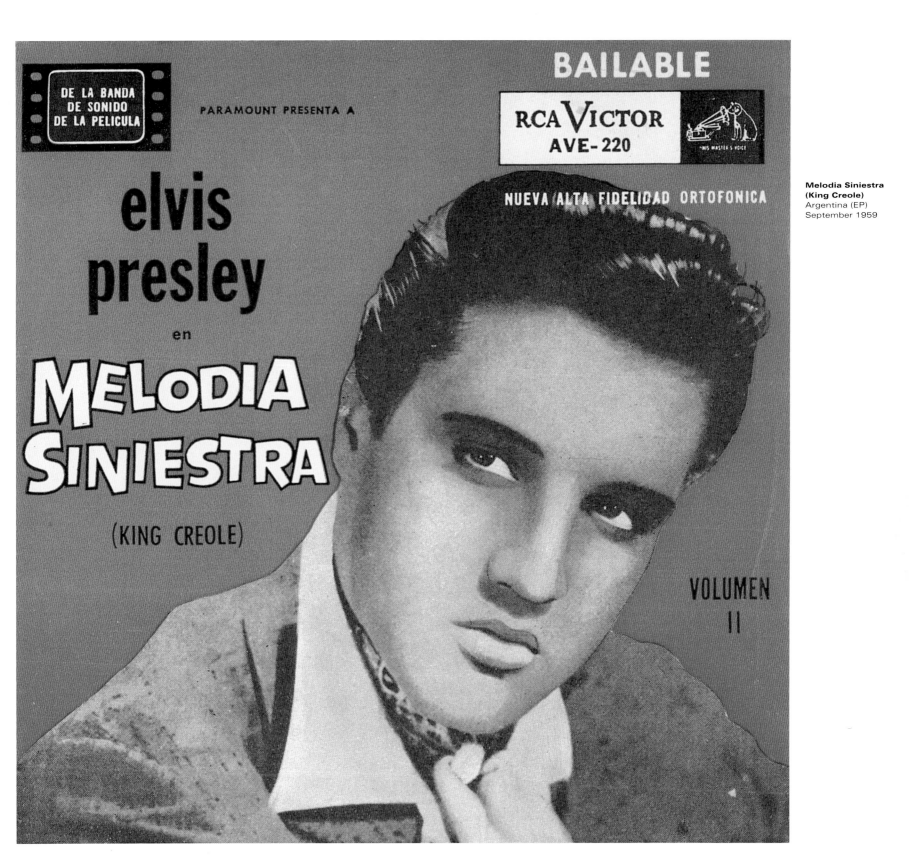

Melodia Siniestra
(King Creole)
Argentina (EP)
September 1959

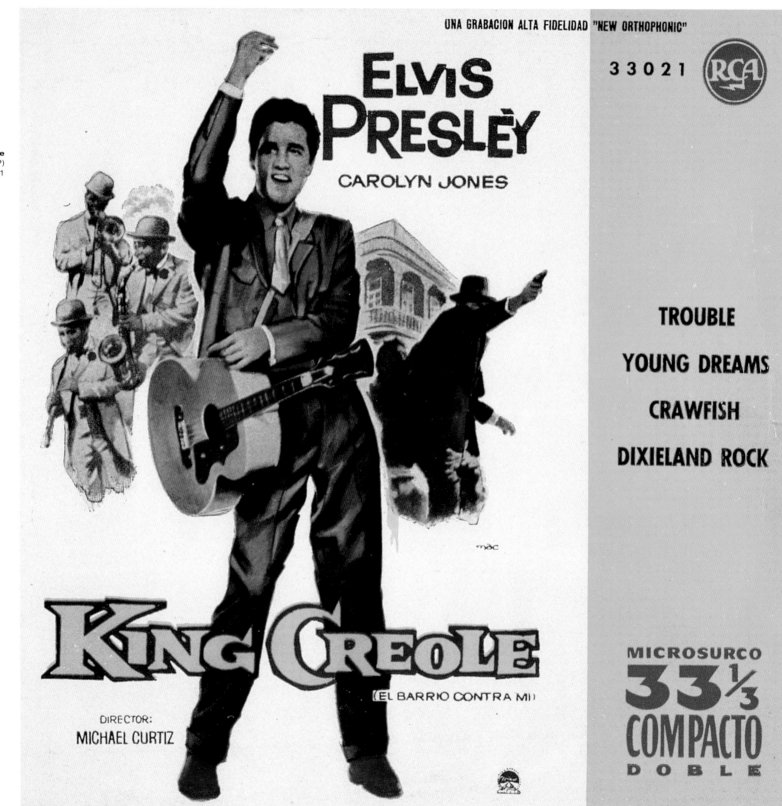

PRESLEY GOLDEN COMPACT SERIES

SCP-1244

闇に響く声/エルヴィス・プレスリー！

キング・クレオール
ニュー・オーリンズ

きみと生きる限り
ラヴァー・ドル

VICTOR
"HIS MASTER'S VOICE"

King Creole
Japan (EP)
December 1965

The Gold Suit

Elvis wearing his gold lamé suit is among the most memorable images from the 1950s. The suit was designed by Liberace's designer, Nudie of Hollywood, in 1957. It supposedly cost $10,000. He wore the suit only a few times in concert—it was heavy and uncomfortable and he hated it. However, the suit gained worldwide attention when it appeared on the cover of the second "Gold Records" LP, titled 50,000,000 Elvis Fans Can't Be Wrong, in 1959 (opposite). By the time RCA released the LP in Argentina three years later (right), it was wisely figured that the number of Elvis fans had doubled. The 1986 Argentinian reissue (page 60) used the original back cover as the front.

Los discos de oro de Presley:
100,000,000 de admiradores no pueden estar equivocados
Argentina (LP)
May 1962

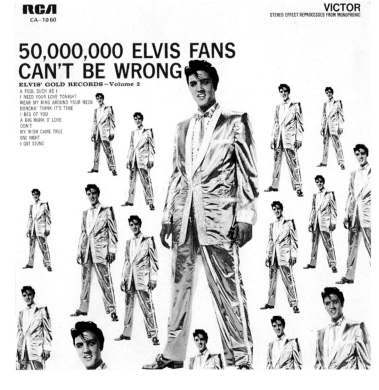

50,000,000 Elvis Fans Can't Be Wrong
El Salvador (LP)
1977

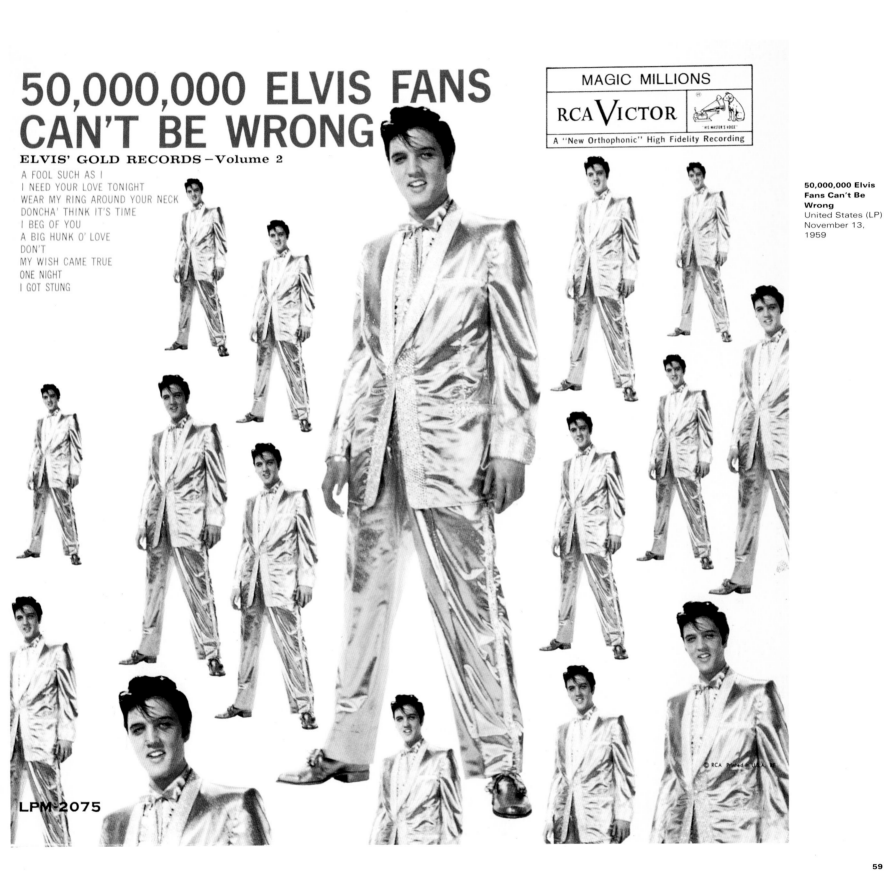

50,000,000 ELVIS FANS CAN'T BE WRONG

ELVIS' GOLD RECORDS — Volume 2

A FOOL SUCH AS I
I NEED YOUR LOVE TONIGHT
WEAR MY RING AROUND YOUR NECK
DONCHA' THINK IT'S TIME
I BEG OF YOU
A BIG HUNK O' LOVE
DON'T
MY WISH CAME TRUE
ONE NIGHT
I GOT STUNG

MAGIC MILLIONS
RCA VICTOR
A "New Orthophonic" High Fidelity Recording

LPM-2075

© RCA Printed in U.S.A.

50,000,000 Elvis Fans Can't Be Wrong
United States (LP)
November 13, 1959

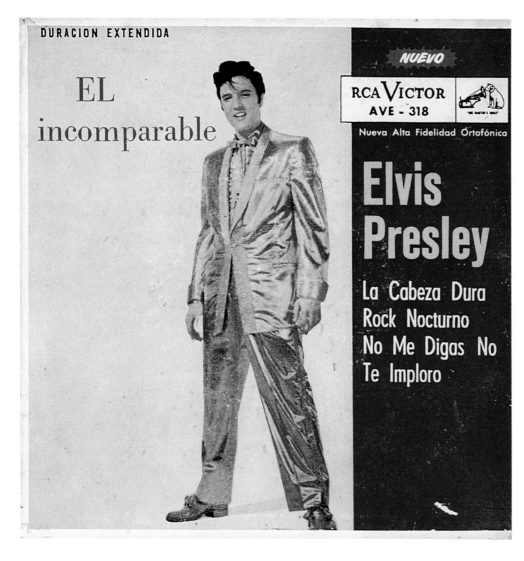

DURACION EXTENDIDA

EL incomparable

NUEVO

RCA VICTOR
AVE - 318

Nueva Alta Fidelidad Ortofónica

Elvis Presley

La Cabeza Dura
Rock Nocturno
No Me Digas No
Te Imploro

El incomparable
Uruguay (EP)
1960

Vol. II

LOS DISCOS
DE ORO DE
ELVIS

(50.000.000
DE FANATICOS NO
PUEDEN
EQUIVOCARSE)

UN TONTO COMO YO
NECESITO TU AMOR ESTA NOCHE
USA MI ANILLO ALREDEDOR
DE TU CUELLO
NO CREES QUE YA ES HORA
TE LO RUEGO
UN GRAN PEDAZO DE AMOR
NO LO HAGAS
MI DESEO SE HIZO REALIDAD
UNA NOCHE
BE PICO

GRABACIONES ORIGINALES
REMATRIZADAS DIGITALMENTE

**Los Discos de
Oro de Elvis**
Argentina (LP)
August 1986

A Date with Elvis

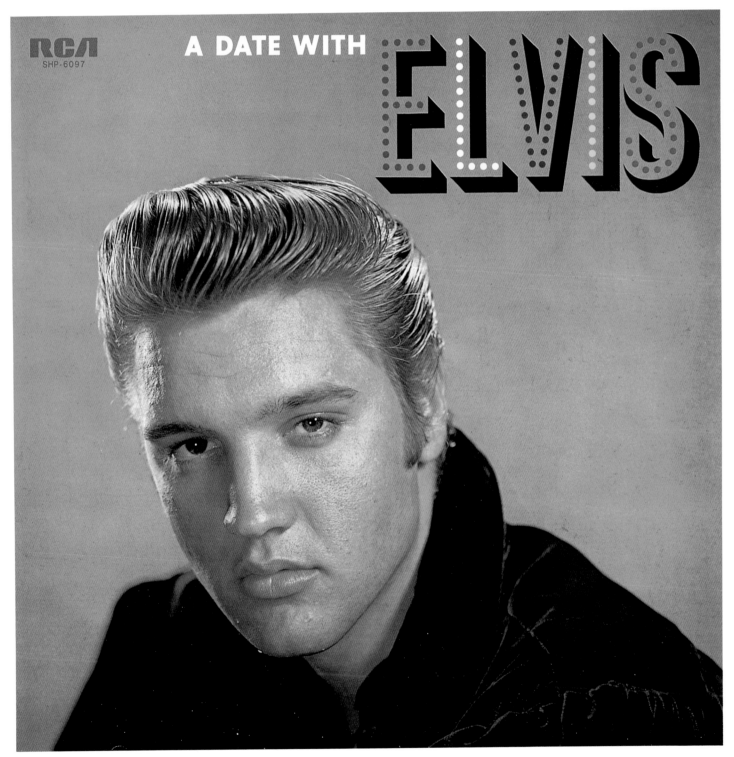

A Date with Elvis
Japan (LP)
April 1970

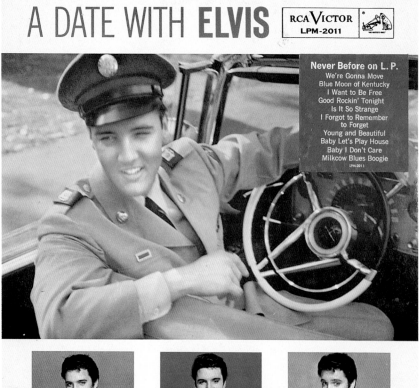

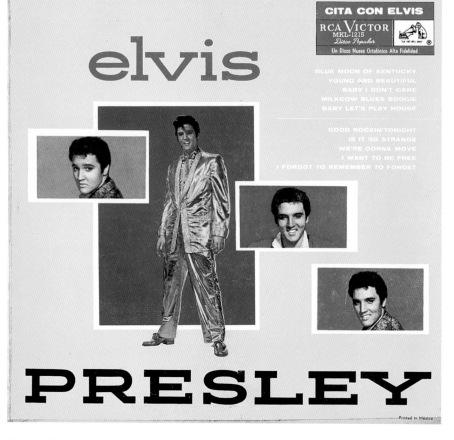

A Date with Elvis
United States (LP)
August 21, 1959

Cita con Elvis
Mexico (LP)
1959

Profiles

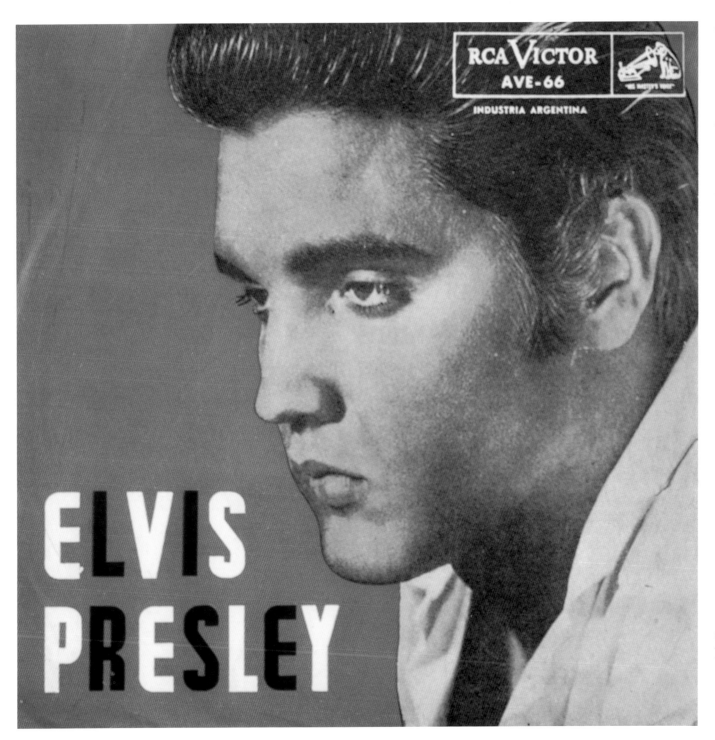

ELVIS PRESLEY

RCA VICTOR
AVE-66
INDUSTRIA ARGENTINA

A typical 1950s design for an Elvis cover included a "profile" shot, used extensively in just about every country. This design scheme became popular again for 1980s and '90s reissues. The latest example shown here (page 64), from 1991, was issued on the first Elvis LP that RCA released in China.

Elvis Presley
Argentina (EP)
June 1958

Elvis' Golden
Records
China (LP)
1991

RCA

Elvis Presley

ELVIS' GOLDEN RECORDS

HOUND DOG
LOVING YOU
ALL SHOOK UP
HEARTBREAK HOTEL
JAILHOUSE ROCK
LOVE ME
TOO MUCH
DON'T BE CRUEL
THAT'S WHEN YOUR HEARTACHES BEGIN
LET ME BE YOUR TEDDY BEAR
LOVE ME TENDER
TREAT ME NICE
ANY WAY YOU WANT ME
I WANT YOU, I NEED YOU, I LOVE YOU

K 音乐娱乐香港有限公司授权
中国广播音像出版社出版
中国唱片总公司上海公司生产发行

JDLH·9102
BMPL·003

广录进字第334号

BMG

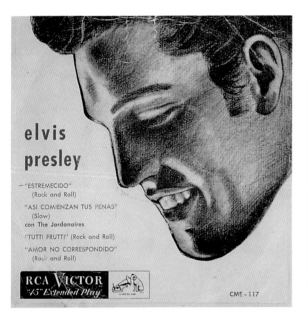

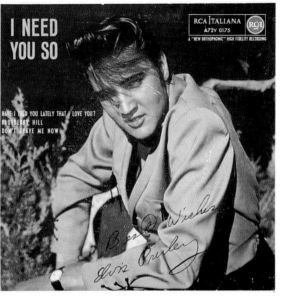

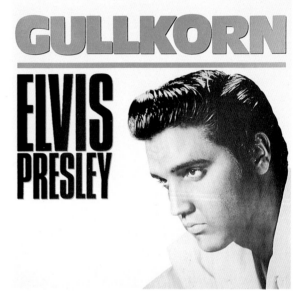

Elvis Presley
Chile (EP)
1957

I Need You So
Italy (EP)
October 1957

Gullkorn
Iceland (LP)
1986

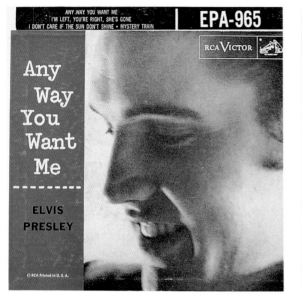

Any Way You Want Me
United States (EP)
September 21, 1956

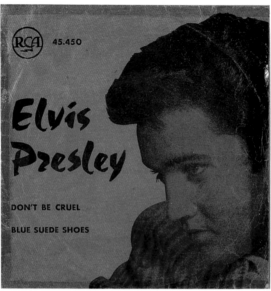

Don't Be Cruel /
Blue Suede Shoes
France (single)
1959

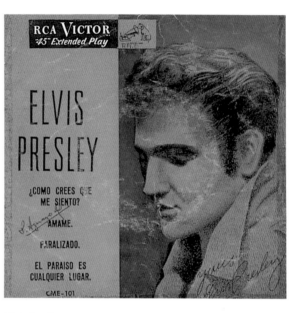

Elvis Presley
Chile (EP)
1957

ELVIS

COMPACT 33 DOUBLE

LPC-3143

"New Orthophonic" High Fidelity Recording

RCA

CUELGA MI ANILLO EN TU CUELLO

¿NO CREES QUE ES TIEMPO?

UN TONTO COMO YO

NECESITO TU AMOR

PRESLEY

Elvis Presley
Spain (EP)
1961

Christmas

The original U.S. Christmas album, released in 1957, was (and still is) the ultimate Elvis package that RCA ever produced in the United States. Inside the cover was a ten-page portfolio of striking color photographs. This format was only available until October 1959, when the record was repackaged in a single sleeve with a different cover. Most Christmas records were on sale for only a short time; therefore, they are hard to come by today. The singles, EPs, and LPs pictured here are among the rarest Elvis records in the world.

Elvis' Christmas Album
Japan (LP)
November 1957

**Here Comes Santa Claus /
Santa Bring My Baby Back**
Japan (single)
October 1965

**Merry Christmas—
Elvis Presley**
Uruguay (EP)
1958

**Elvis' Christmas
Album**
United States (LP)
October 15, 1957

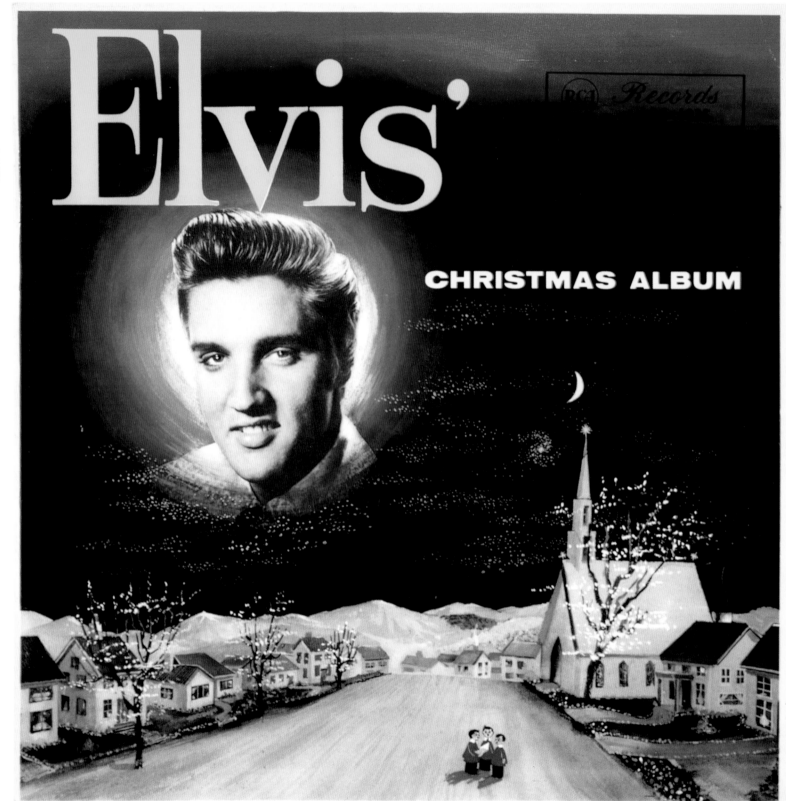

Elvis' Christmas
Album
New Zealand (LP)
1957

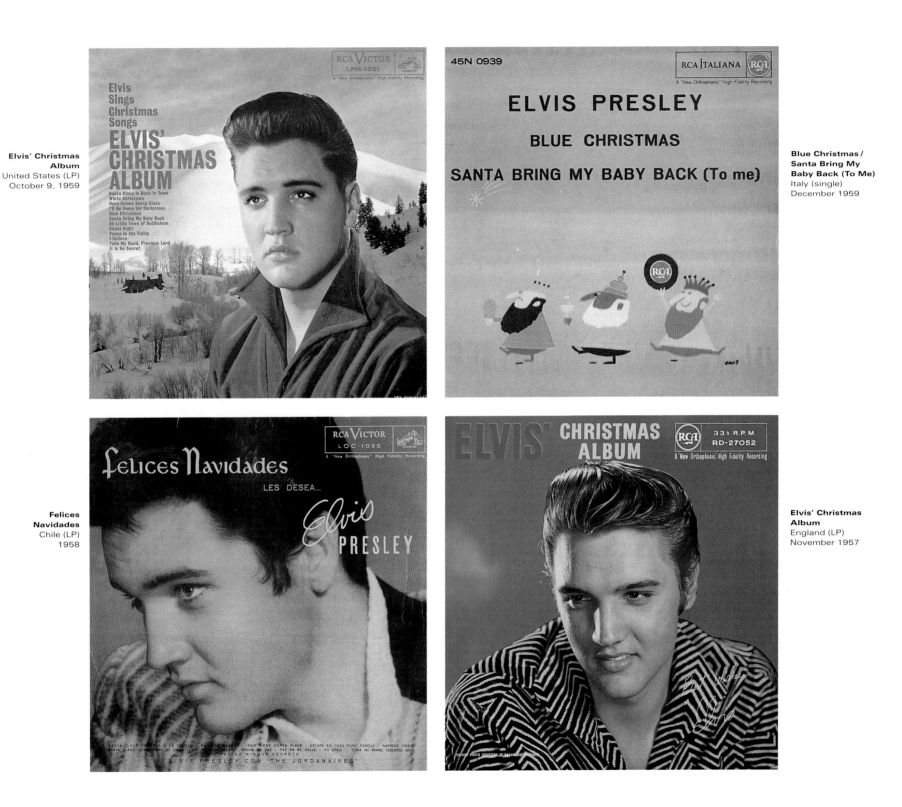

Elvis' Christmas Album
United States (LP)
October 9, 1959

Blue Christmas / Santa Bring My Baby Back (To Me)
Italy (single)
December 1959

Felices Navidades
Chile (LP)
1958

Elvis' Christmas Album
England (LP)
November 1957

Elvis in the Army

There were no songs on the Elvis Sails EP, just interviews with Elvis while on board a ship heading for Germany. The 1959 single "A Big Hunk O' Love" was recorded a year earlier during an army leave.

Elvis Sails
Japan (EP)
January 1959

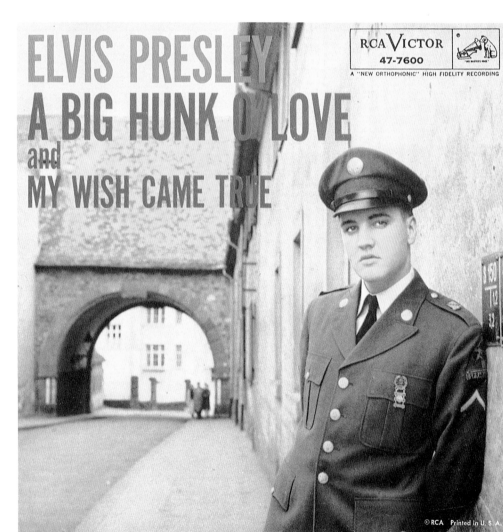

**A Big Hunk O' Love /
My Wish Came True**
United States (single)
June 23, 1959

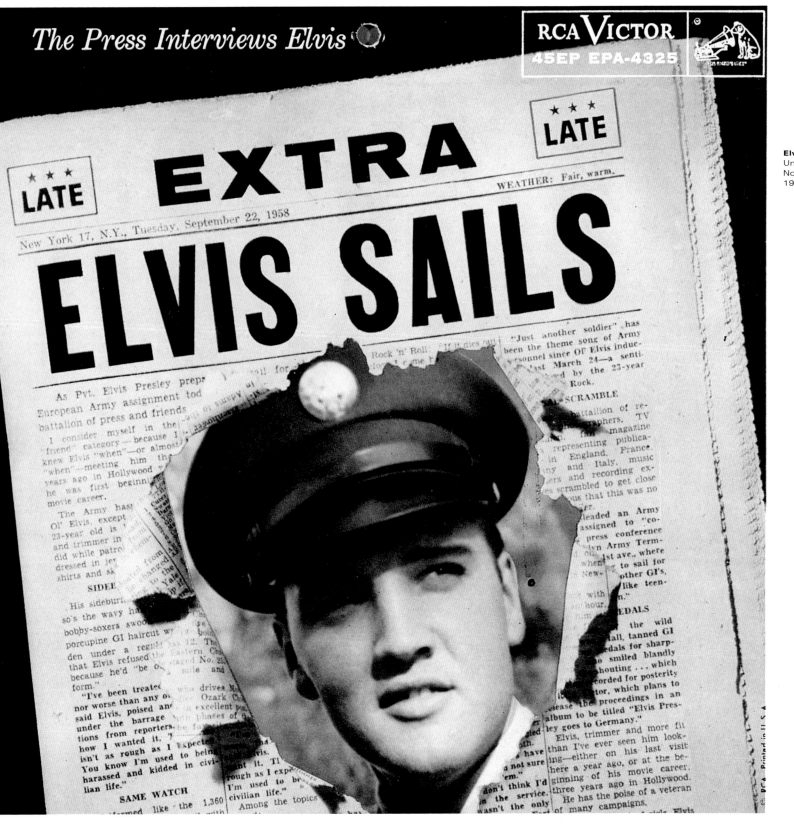

The Press Interviews Elvis

RCA VICTOR
45EP EPA-4325

EXTRA
★★★ LATE   LATE ★★★

ELVIS SAILS

New York 17, N.Y., Tuesday, September 22, 1958

WEATHER: Fair, warm.

Elvis Sails
United States (EP)
November 18, 1958

73

THE

196s

Elvis Is Back

430.324
(LPM 2231)
STANDARD

RCA

LE RETOUR D' ELVIS

A "New Orthophonic" High Fidelity Recording

RCA issued records in several countries to celebrate Elvis's return from the army and to capitalize on his popular reception at home and abroad. The French LP, Le Retour d'Elvis, *was available with this cover for only one month, after which it was released in the same cover as that used on the original U.S. issue.*

Le Retour d'Elvis
France (LP)
May 1960

Elvis Is Back!
United States (LP)
April 8, 1960

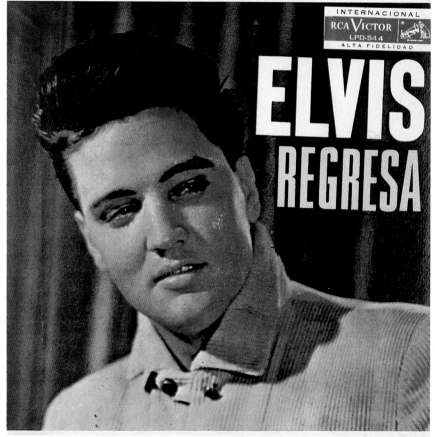

Elvis Regresa
(Elvis Is Back)
Cuba (LP)
1960

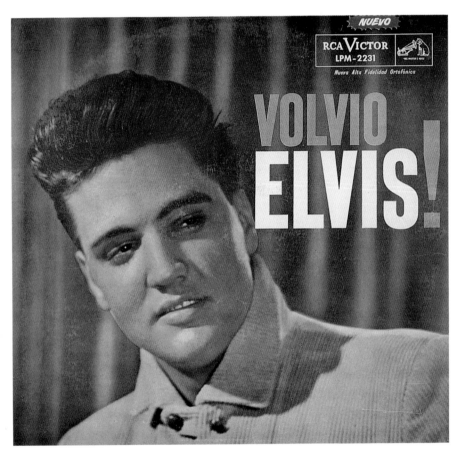

Volvio Elvis! (Elvis Is Back!)
Argentina (LP)
July 1960

BLUE SUEDE SHOES

I'M COUNTING ON YOU

I GOT A WOMAN

ONE SIDED LOVE AFFAIR

I LOVE YOU BECAUSE

JUST BECAUSE

TUTTI FRUTTI

TRYIN' TO GET TO YOU

I'M GONNA SIT RIGHT DOWN AND CRY
(Over You)

I'LL NEVER LET YOU GO

BLUE MOON

MONEY HONEY

Elvis Presley
Colombia (LP)
1965

It's Now or Never

**O Sole Mio
(It's Now or Never) /
Make Me Know It**
Denmark (single)
1960

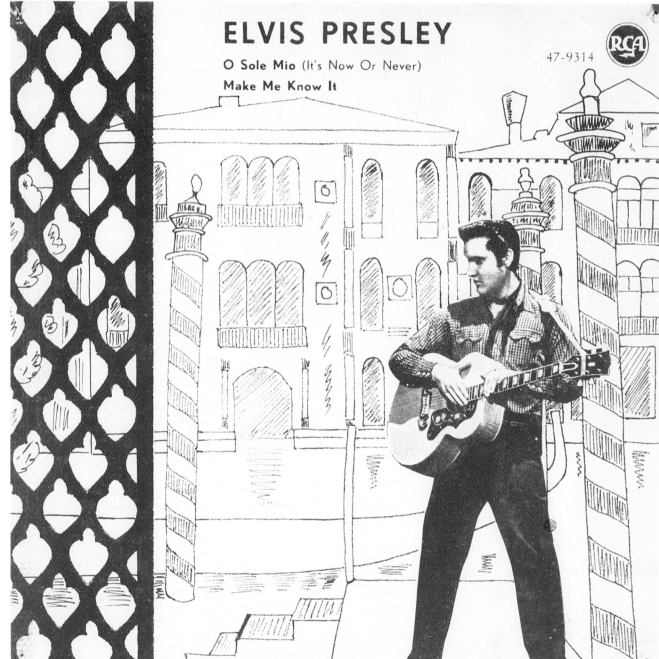

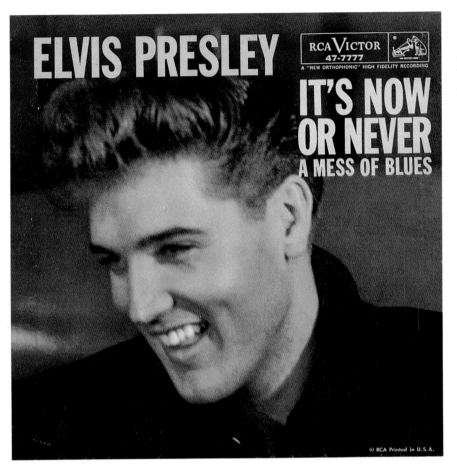

It's Now or Never /
A Mess of Blues
United States (single)
July 5, 1960

It's Now or Never /
Make Me Know It
Italy (single)
1960

Surrender

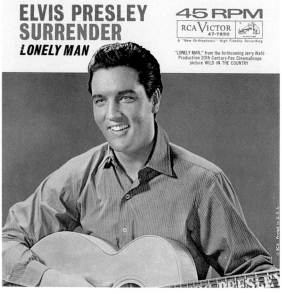

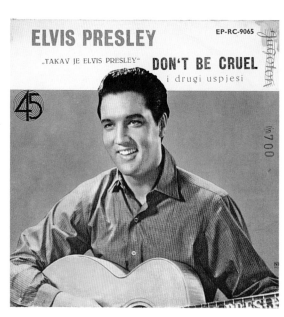

Surrender / Lonely Man
United States (single)
February 7, 1961

Takav Je Elvis Presley
(Don't Be Cruel)
Yugoslavia (EP)
1961

Torna a Surriento
(Surrender) / Lonely Man
Italy (single)
August 1961

King of the Whole Wide World

First, Elvis was crowned the King of Rock 'n' Roll, but it was not long before he had conquered the world. The title of the rare South African LP that first made this claim was taken from a song in the Kid Galahad *movie.*

One World One King
Hong Kong (LP)
1988

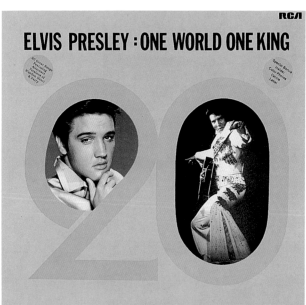

King of the Whole Wide World
South Africa (LP)
1962

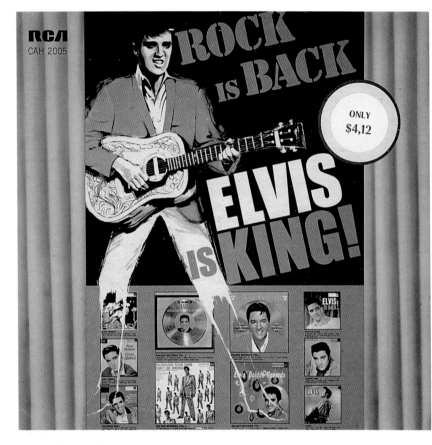

**Rock Is Back—
Elvis Is King!**
South Africa (LP)
1968

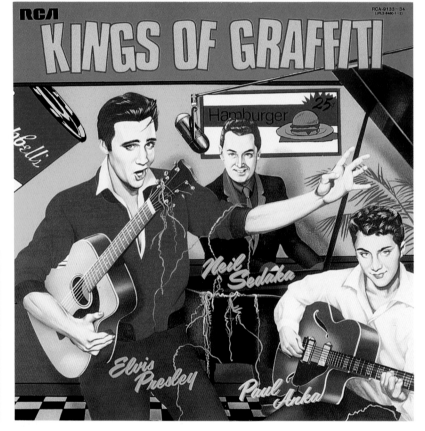

Kings of Graffiti
Japan (LP)
October 1977

Good Luck Charm

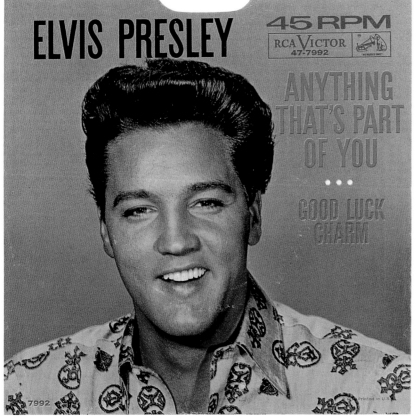

**Anything That's
Part of You / Good
Luck Charm**
United States (single)
October 1962

**Portafortuna
(Good Luck Charm)**
Italy (single)
1962

Golden Records

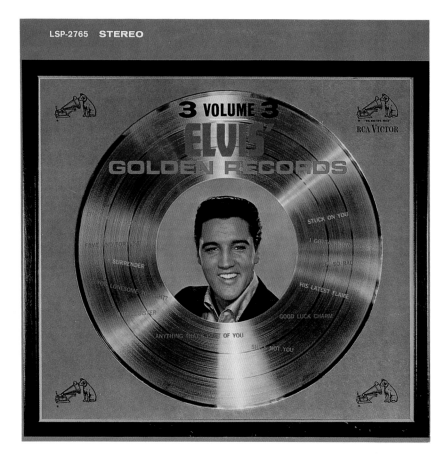

Elvis' Golden Records Vol. 3
United States (LP)
September 1963

Elvis' Golden Records Vol. 3
Japan (LP)
August 1963

Four volumes of Elvis' Golden Records *were released between 1958 and 1968. The Japanese version of volume three is interesting because it was issued one month before the U.S. LP and with a much different cover design.*

Elvis for Everyone

Elvis for Everyone!
United States (LP)
July 1965

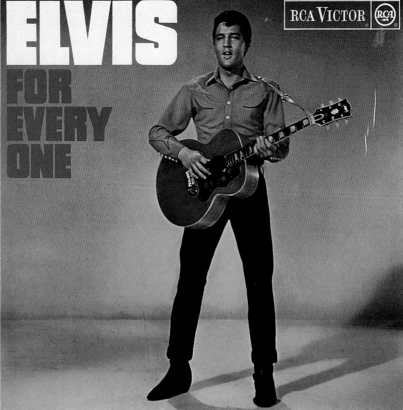

Elvis for Everyone
England (LP)
November 1965

Big Boss Man

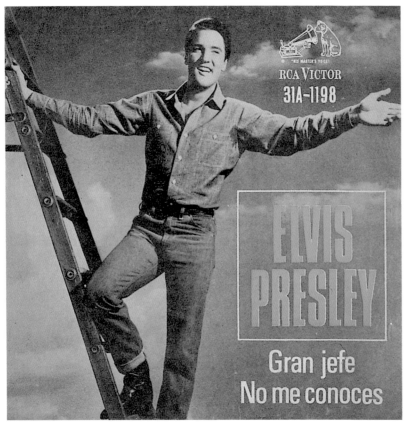

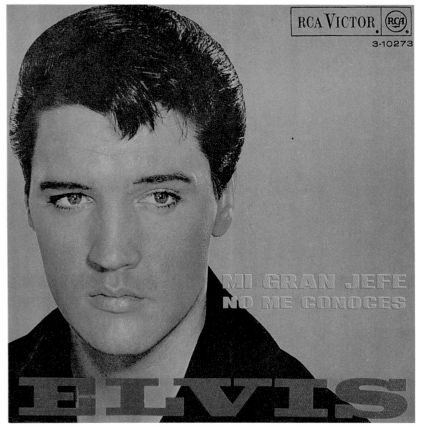

**Big Boss Man /
You Don't Know Me**
Argentina (single)
November 1967

**Big Boss Man /
You Don't Know Me**
Spain (single)
1968

Gospel

His Hand in Mine
United States (LP)
November 23, 1960

Gospel was Elvis's favorite musical genre, and he sang it throughout his life. The first of his several gospel records was released in 1960.

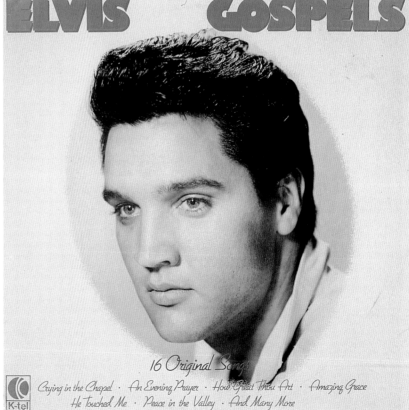

Elvis Gospels
Sweden (LP)
1980

The Comeback

By 1968 Elvis was becoming a relic in the music world, having devoted the better part of the decade to his movie career. His historic "comeback" performance on TV and the accompanying soundtrack LP introduced a new image for the performer. The show featured the new original song "If I Can Dream" written specifically for Elvis. It was also released as a single.

**If I Can Dream /
Memories**
United States (single)
November 1968

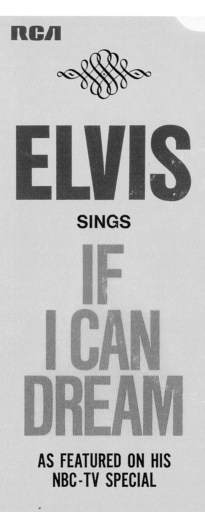

**If I Can Dream /
Edge of Reality**
Japan (single)
February 1969

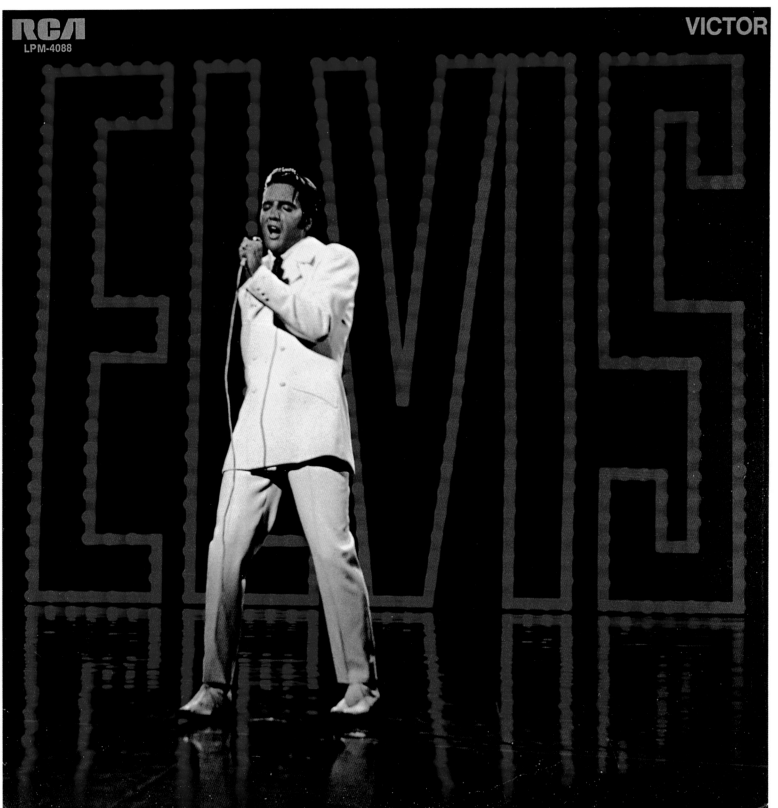

RCA
LPM-4088

VICTOR

**Elvis NBC TV
Special**
United States (LP)
November 25, 1968

Suspicious Minds

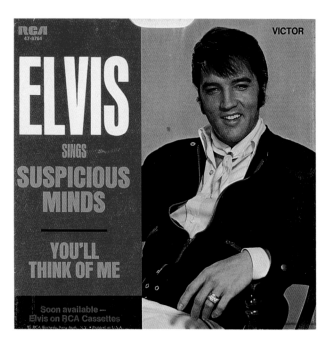

**Suspicious Minds /
You'll Think of Me**
United States (single)
August 1969

**Suspicious Minds /
You'll Think of Me**
Turkey (single)
1969

Don't Cry Daddy

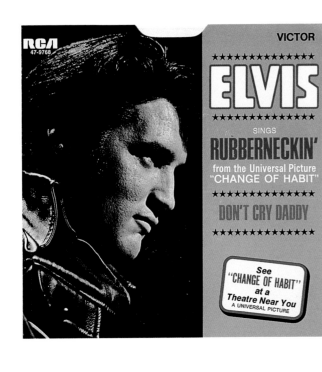

**Rubberneckin' /
Don't Cry Daddy**
United States (single)
December 2, 1969

**Don't Cry Daddy /
Rubberneckin'**
Turkey (single)
1969

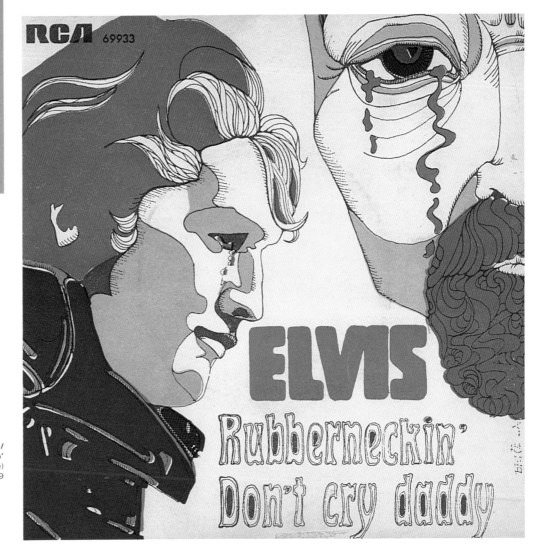

From Memphis to Vegas

From Memphis to Vegas
United States (LP)
November 16, 1969

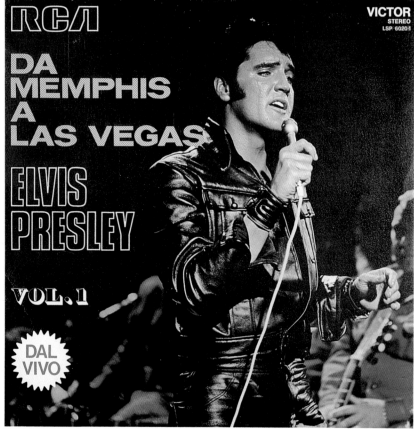

**Da Memphis a
Las Vegas Vol. 1**
Italy (LP)
1970

LSP-4155

VICTOR
STEREO

From Elvis in Memphis
United States (LP)
June 1969

THE

1960s

SOUNDTRACKS

G.I. Blues

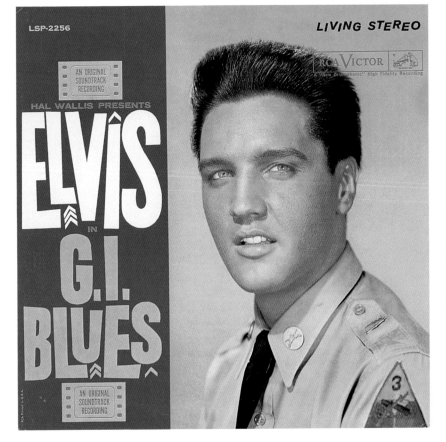

G.I. Blues
United States (LP)
September 23, 1960

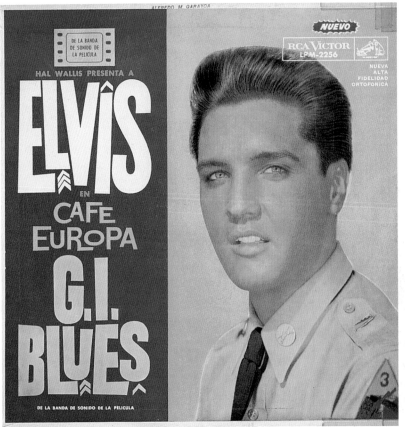

Cafe Europa (G.I. Blues)
Argentina (LP)
April 1961

Twenty-seven of Elvis's thirty-three movies, which varied in title from country to country, were made in the 1960s. Publicity photos, movie stills, lobby cards, posters, and the like provided a seemingly endless number of images available for soundtrack covers.

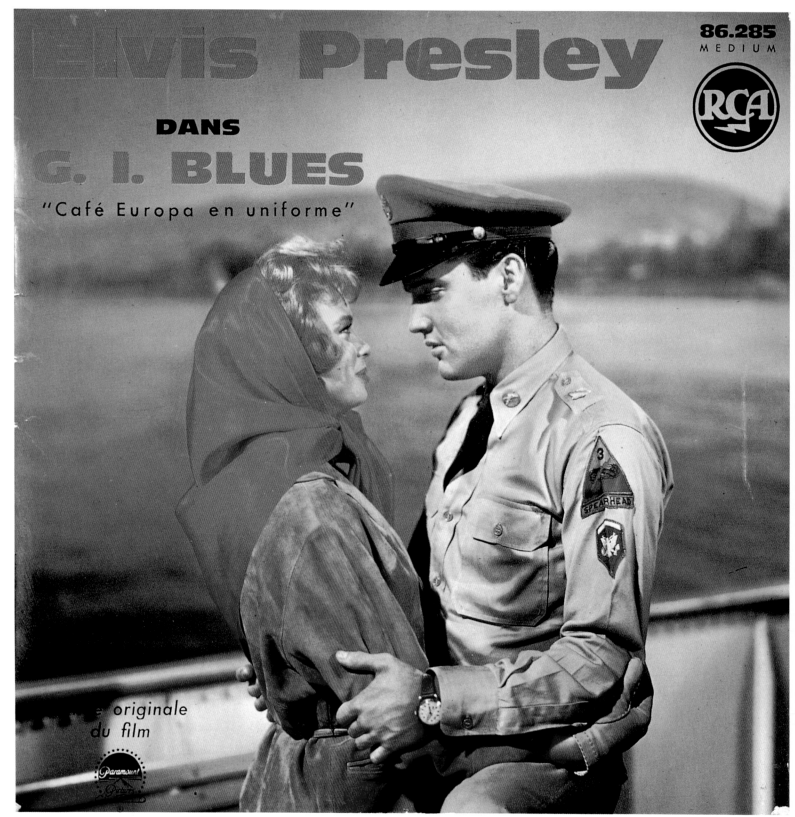

**Café Europa
(G.I. Blues)**
France (EP)
February 1961

Blue Hawaii

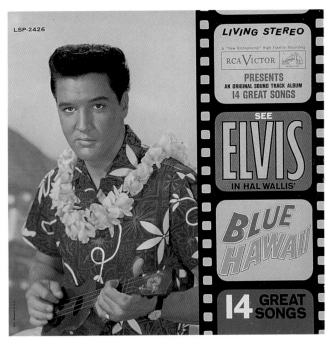

Blue Hawaii
United States (LP)
October 20, 1961

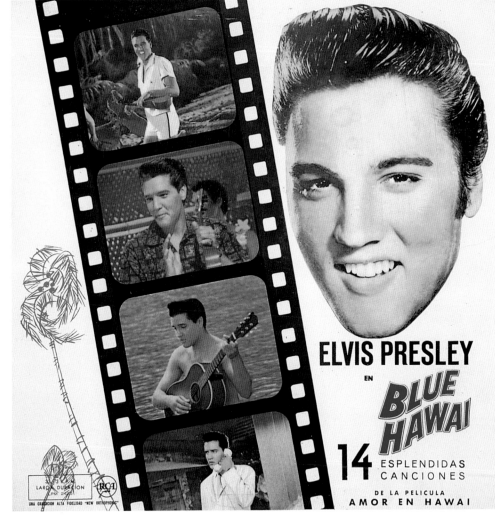

Blue Hawaii
Spain (LP)
1961

Follow That Dream

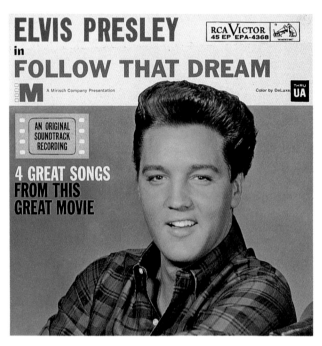

Follow That Dream
United States (EP)
April 1962

Follow That Dream
Japan (EP)
December 1965

Kid Galahad

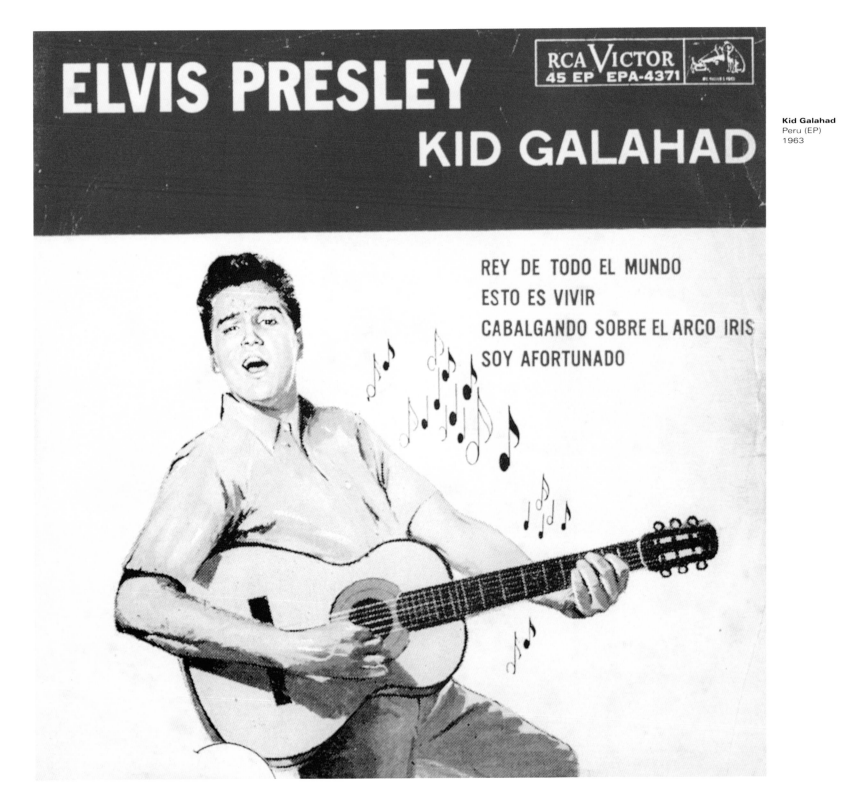

Kid Galahad
Peru (EP)
1963

PRESLEY GOLDEN COMPACT SERIES

SCP-1247

「恋のKOパンチ」

～ユナイト映画「恋のKOパンチ」
オリジナル・サウンドトラックより

唄）
エルヴィス・プレスリー

広い世界のチャンピオン
これが暮しだ
虹に乗って
愛が住み家
アイ・ガット・ラッキー
口笛吹いて

VICTOR
"HIS MASTER'S VOICE"

Kid Galahad
Japan (EP)
December 1965

ELVIS PRESLEY
in KID GALAHAD

RCA VICTOR
45 EP EPA-4371

A Mirisch Company Production

Color by Deluxe

THRU UA

AN ORIGINAL SOUNDTRACK RECORDING

SIX GREAT SONGS

King of the Whole Wide World
This Is Living
Riding the Rainbow
Home Is Where the Heart Is
I Got Lucky
A Whistling Tune

Kid Galahad
United States (EP)
August 21, 1962

Girls! Girls! Girls!

Girls! Girls! Girls!
United States (LP)
November 12, 1962

Chicas! Chicas! Chicas!
Uruguay (LP)
April 1963

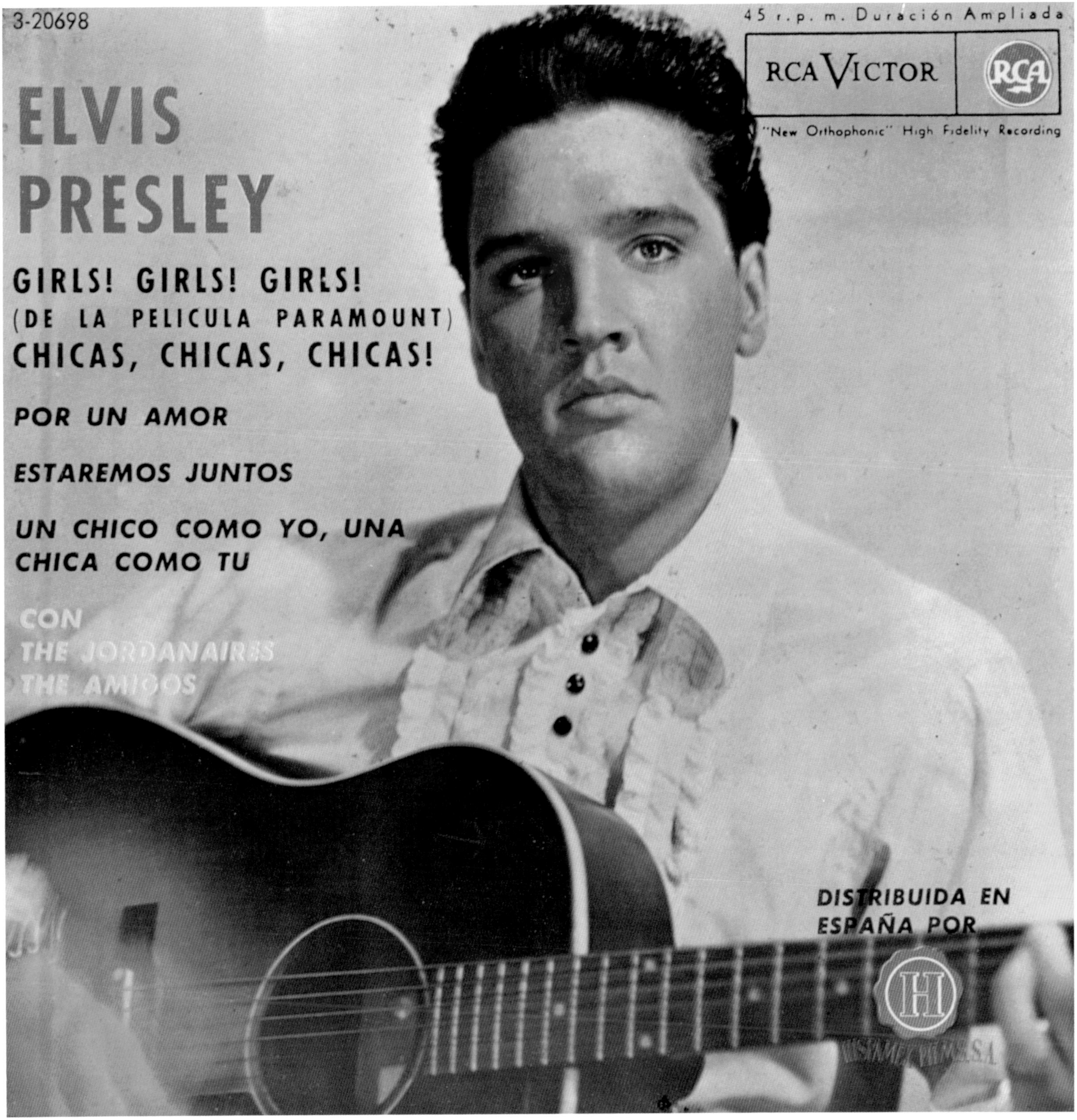

Girls! Girls! Girls!
Spain (EP)
1963

It Happened at the World's Fair

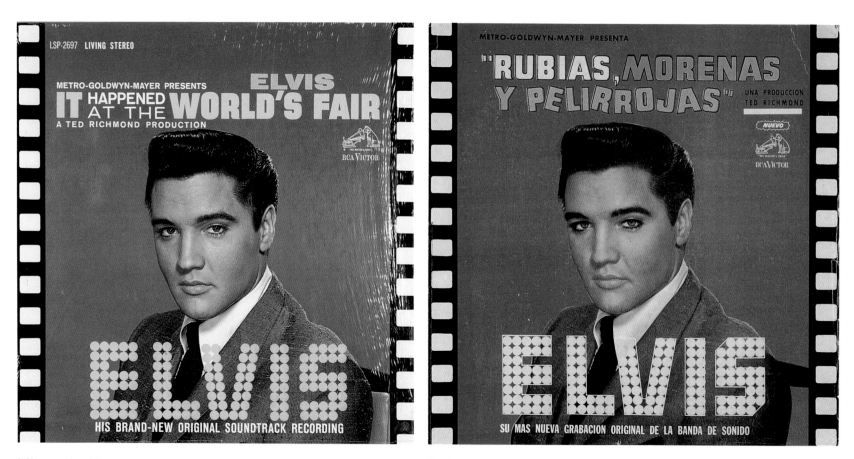

**It Happened at the
World's Fair**
United States (LP)
April 1963

**Rubias, Morenas y
Pelirrojas (It Happened
at the World's Fair)**
Argentina (LP)
August 1963

COLONNA SONORA DEL FILM
Metro-Goldwyn-Mayer

BIONDE, ROSSE, BRUNE...

(IT HAPPENED AT THE WORLD'S FAIR)

ELVIS PRESLEY

RCA

Bionde, Rosse,
Brune . . .
(It Happened at
the World's Fair)
Italy (LP)
1982

Fun in Acapulco

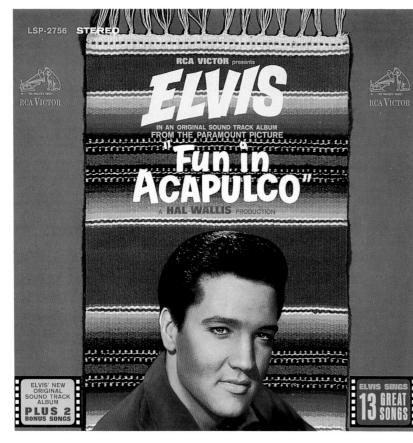

Fun in Acapulco
United States (LP)
November 15, 1963

**Bossa Nova Baby /
Vino, Dinero y Amor**
Peru (single)
January 1964

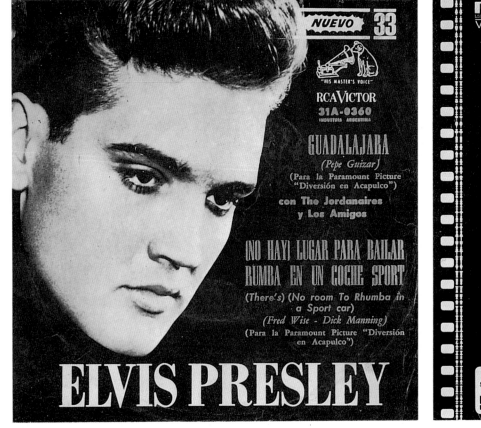

**Guadalajara / There's No Room
to Rhumba in a Sports Car**
Argentina (single)
1964

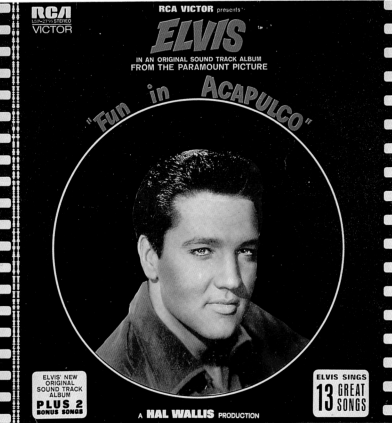

Fun in Acapulco
Israel (LP)
1973

Kissin' Cousins

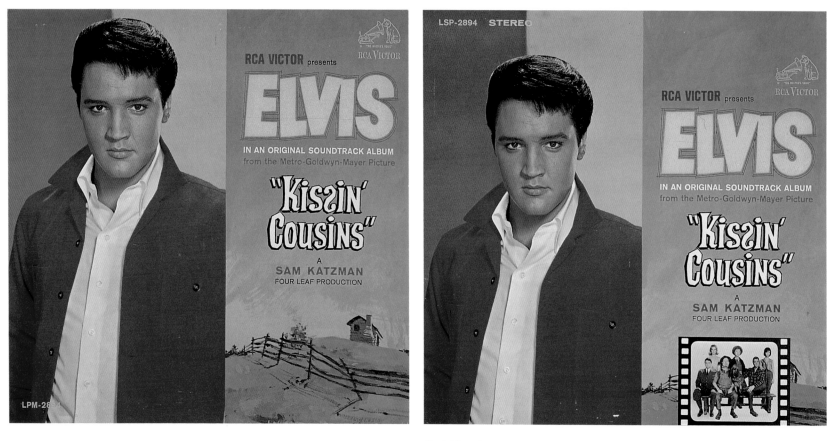

Kissin' Cousins
United States (LP)
April 1964

Kissin' Cousins
United States (LP)
1965

*RCA in the United States changed the cover of
the* Kissin' Cousins *LP one year after its release in
order to show that Elvis played a dual role in the
movie. The 1964 cover is very rare.*

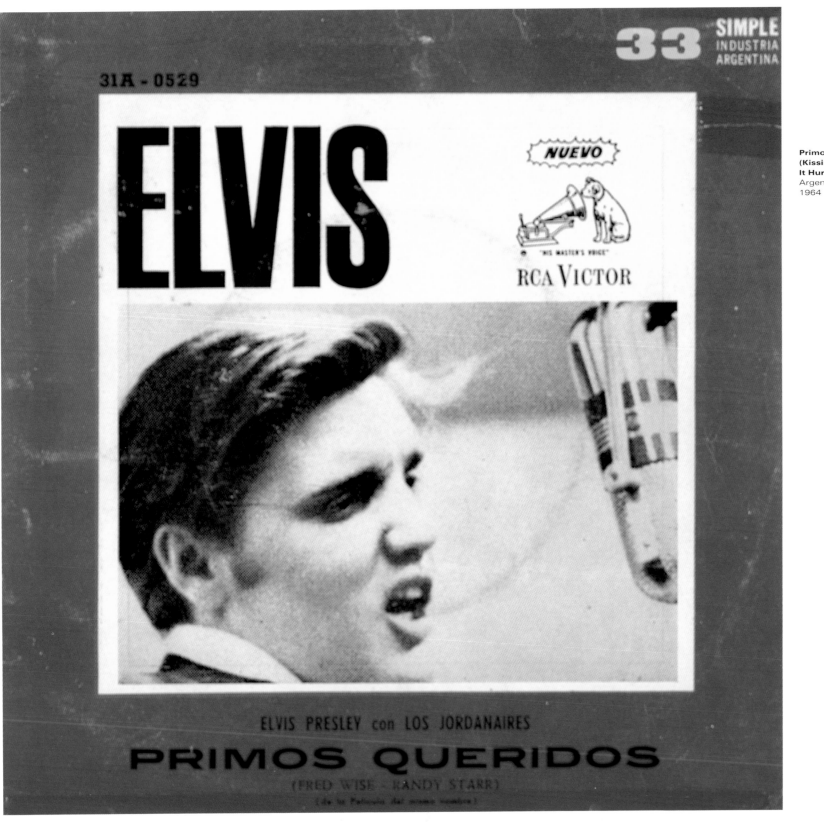

Primos Queridos
(Kissin' Cousins /
It Hurts Me)
Argentina (single)
1964

Viva Las Vegas

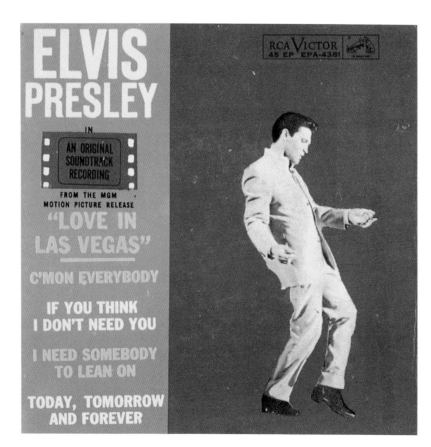

Love in Las Vegas
Philippines (EP)
1964

**C'Mon Everybody /
If You Think I Don't
Need You**
Peru (single)
1964

Viva Las Vegas /
What'd I Say
Brazil (single)
1964

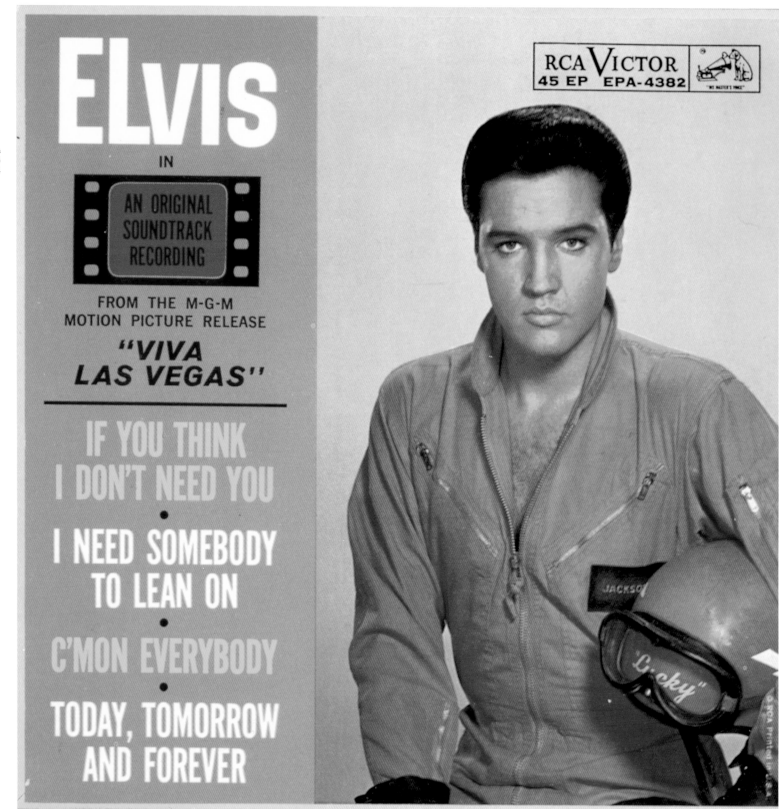

Viva Las Vegas
United States (EP)
June 1964

ELVIS
LOVE IN LAS VEGAS
VOL. 2

Love in Las Vegas
Vol. 2
Australia (EP)
1984

RCA
20666
VICTOR

Roustabout

**Roustabout /
Hard Knocks**
Peru (single)
1964

**El Carrousel del Amor
(Roustabout)**
Argentina (LP)
March 1965

RCA VICTOR
PRESENTS

ELVIS ROUSTABOUT ELVIS

A HAL WALLIS PRODUCTION

THE ORIGINAL SOUNDTRACK ALBUM
FROM THE PARAMOUNT PICTURE
"ROUSTABOUT"

Roustabout
United States (LP)
October 19, 1964

Tickle Me

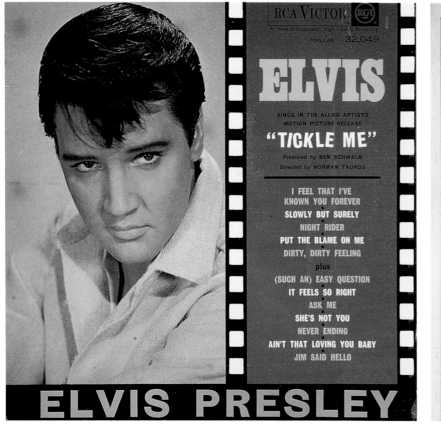

Tickle Me
South Africa (LP)
1965

Tickle Me Vol. 2
Israel (EP)
1965

(It's a) Long
Lonely Highway /
I'm Yours
Japan (single)
September 1965

Girl Happy

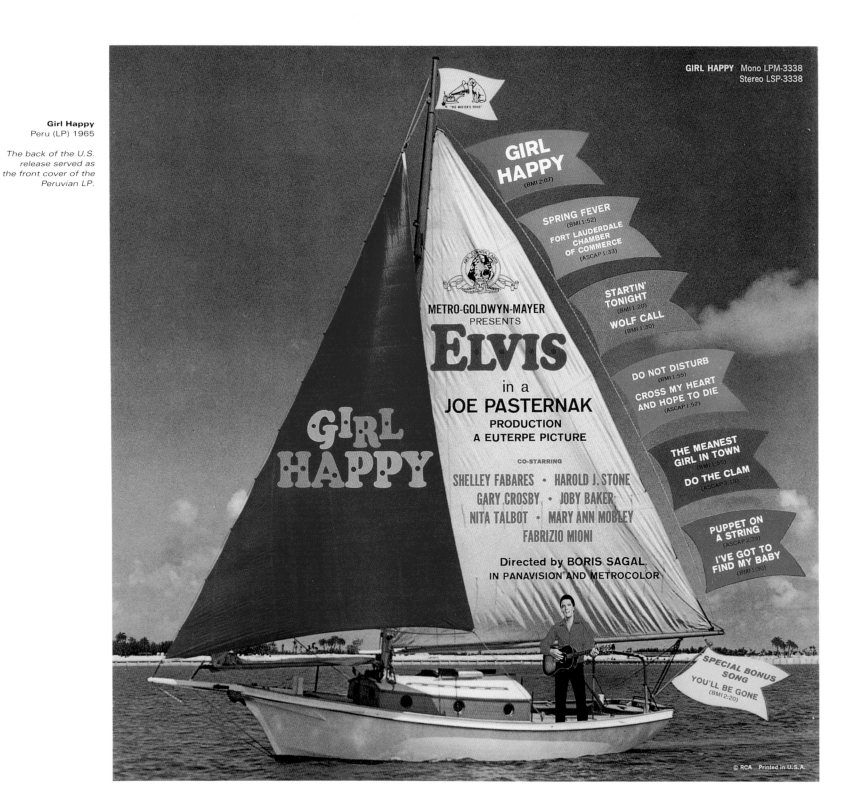

Girl Happy
Peru (LP) 1965

The back of the U.S. release served as the front cover of the Peruvian LP.

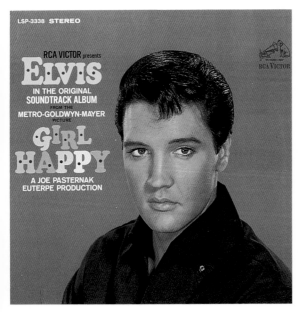

Girl Happy
United States (LP)
March 26, 1965

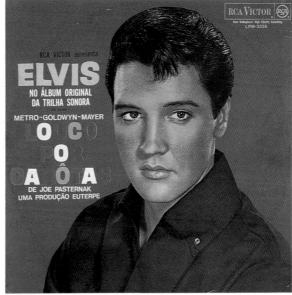

Louco por Garôtas
(Girl Happy)
Brazil (LP)
1965

Girl Happy
Japan (LP)
July 1965

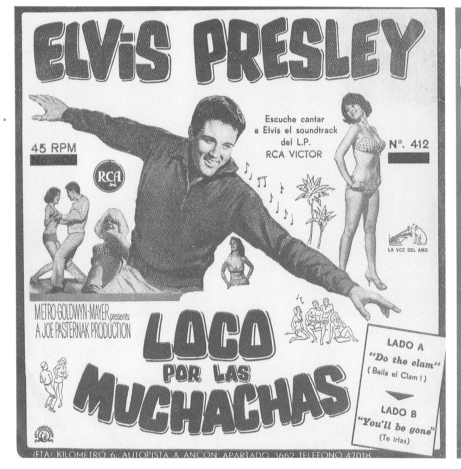

**Loco por las Muchachas
(Do the Clam / You'll Be Gone)**
Peru (single)
1965

Girl Happy
Greece (EP)
1965

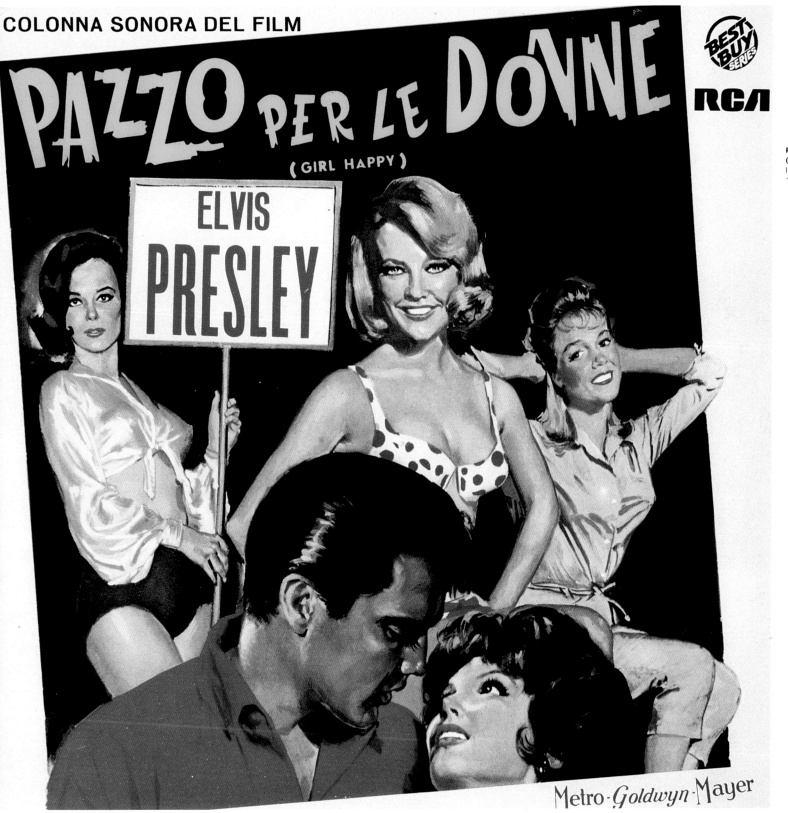

COLONNA SONORA DEL FILM

PAZZO per le DONNE

(GIRL HAPPY)

ELVIS PRESLEY

Best Buy Series

RCA

Metro·Goldwyn·Mayer

**Pazzo per le Donne
(Girl Happy)**
Italy (LP)
1982

Harum Scarum

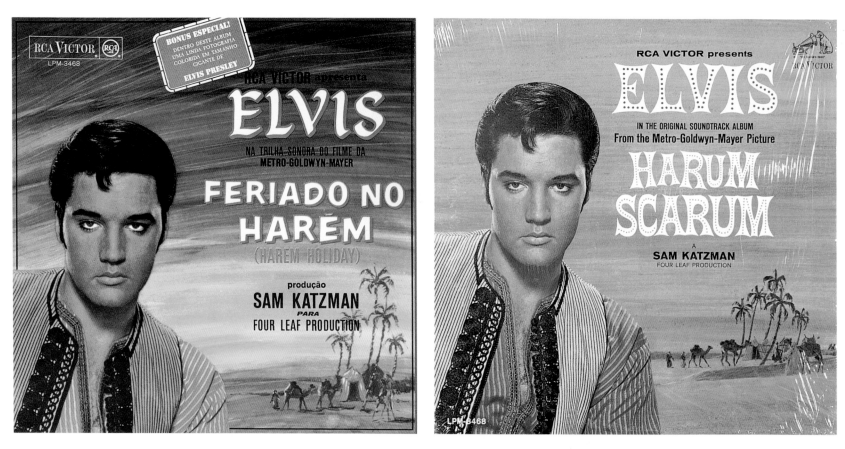

Feriado No Harém
(Harem Holiday)
Brazil (LP)
1966

Harum Scarum
United States (LP)
November 1965

Shake That
Tambourine /
Animal Instinct
Peru (single)
1966

Frankie and Johnny

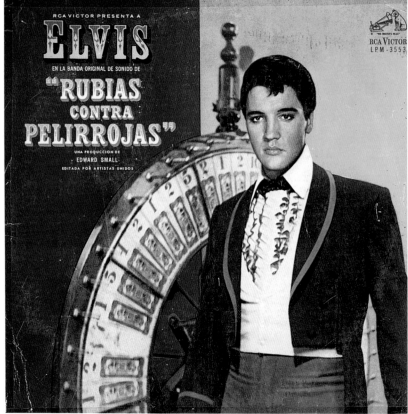

**Frankie and Johnny /
Please Don't Stop Loving Me**
Peru (single)
1966

Rubias Contra Pelirrojas
Argentina (LP)
August 1966

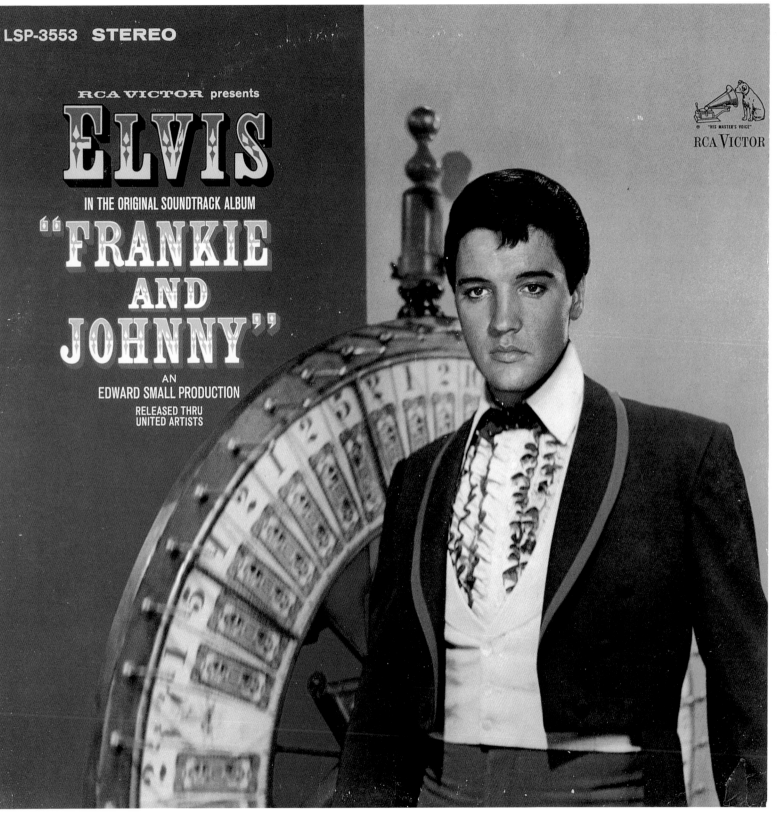

LSP-3553 STEREO

RCA VICTOR presents

ELVIS

IN THE ORIGINAL SOUNDTRACK ALBUM

"FRANKIE AND JOHNNY"

AN
EDWARD SMALL PRODUCTION

RELEASED THRU
UNITED ARTISTS

RCA VICTOR

Frankie and Johnny
United States (LP)
March 21, 1966

Spinout

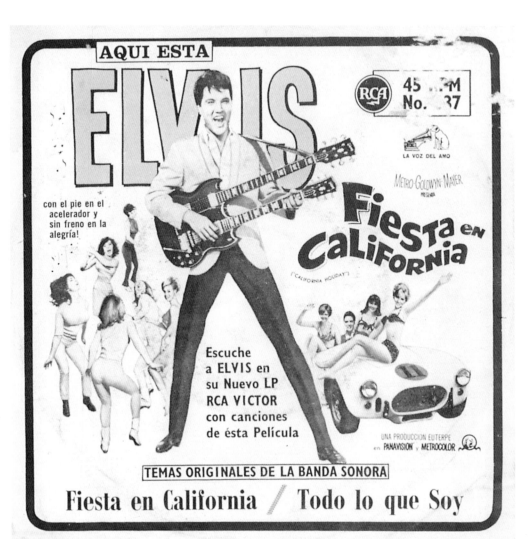

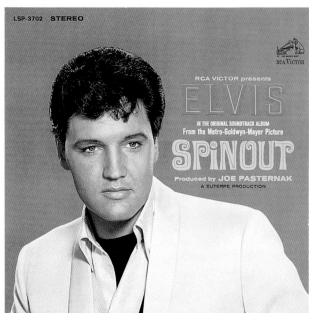

Spinout
United States (LP)
October 24, 1966

Spinout /
All That I Am
Peru (single)
1966

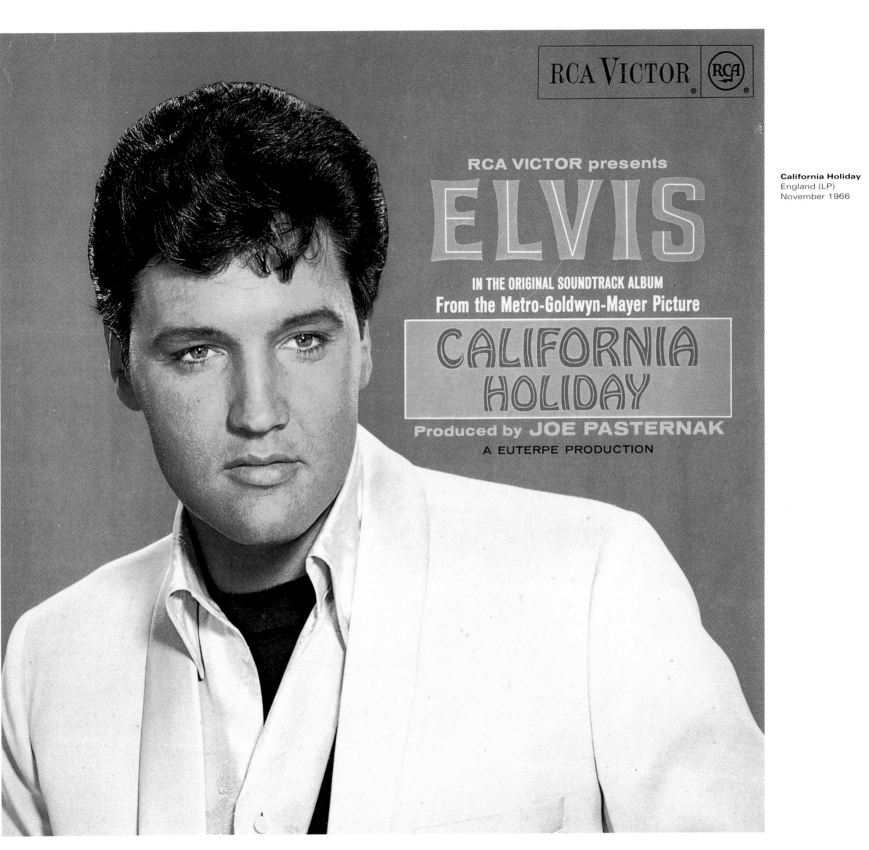

California Holiday
England (LP)
November 1966

Easy Come, Easy Go

It is not just a coincidence that the design of the New Zealand EP See the USA the Elvis Way looks similar to the U.S. Easy Come, Easy Go EP. The former compilation had been scheduled to come out in the United States as Hear the USA the Elvis Way, but that release was scrapped. However, the design concept was retained for this U.S. soundtrack EP.

See the USA the Elvis Way
New Zealand (EP)
March 1967

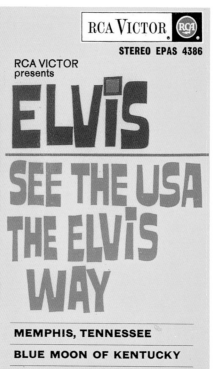

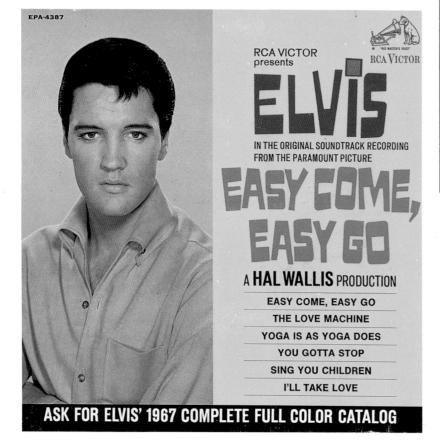

Easy Come, Easy Go
United States (EP)
March 20, 1967

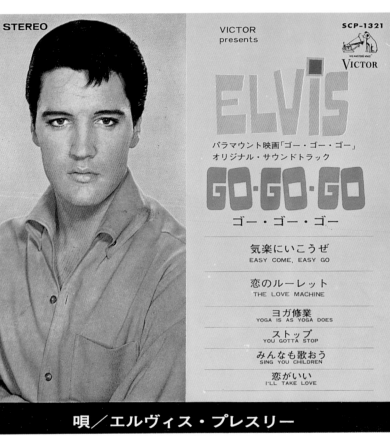

Easy Come, Easy Go
Australia (LP)
May 1967

Go-Go-Go
Japan (EP)
July 1967

Speedway

Speedway
United States (LP)
May 1968

**Let Yourself Go / Your Time
Hasn't Come Yet Baby**
Japan (single)
July 1968

A Tutto Gas
(Speedway)
Italy (LP)
1982

Charro / Memories
Japan (single)
July 1969

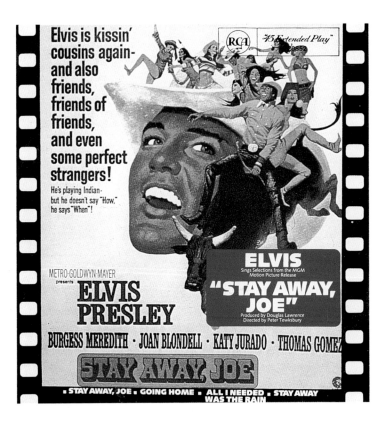

Stay Away, Joe
Australia (EP)
1982

Change of Habit
Australia (EP)
1984

THE 1970s

AND BEYOND

That's the Way It Is

That's the Way It Is was the title of the first film documentary about Elvis. The title was changed on several foreign releases.

That's the Way It Is
United States (LP)
November 1970

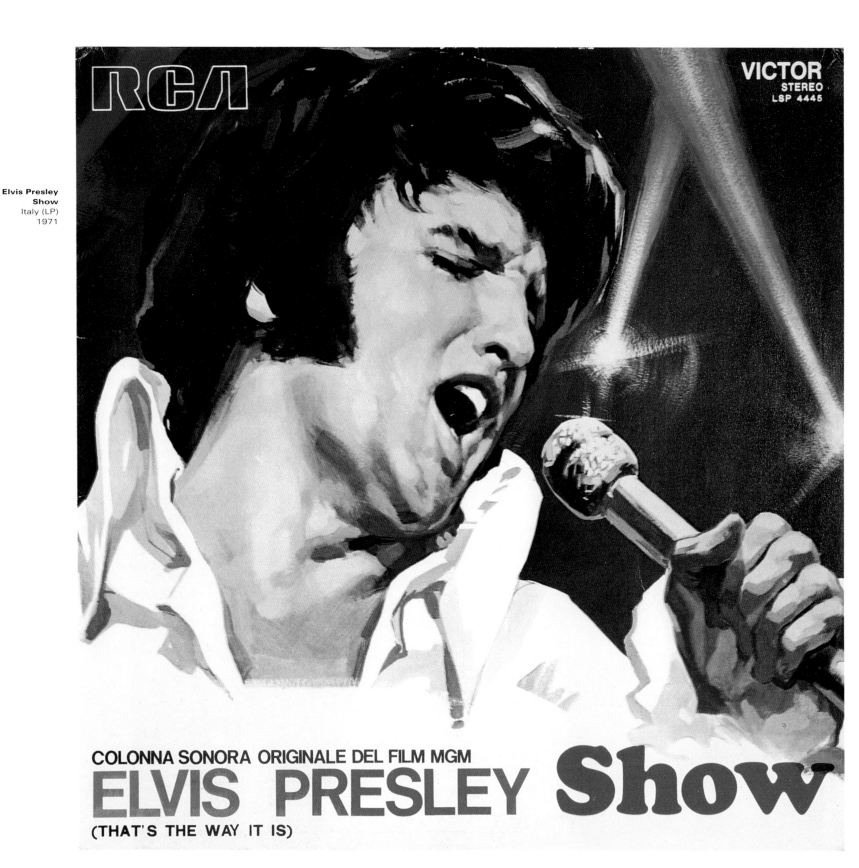

Elvis Presley
Show
Italy (LP)
1971

RCA

VICTOR
STEREO
LSP 4445

COLONNA SONORA ORIGINALE DEL FILM MGM
ELVIS PRESLEY Show
(THAT'S THE WAY IT IS)

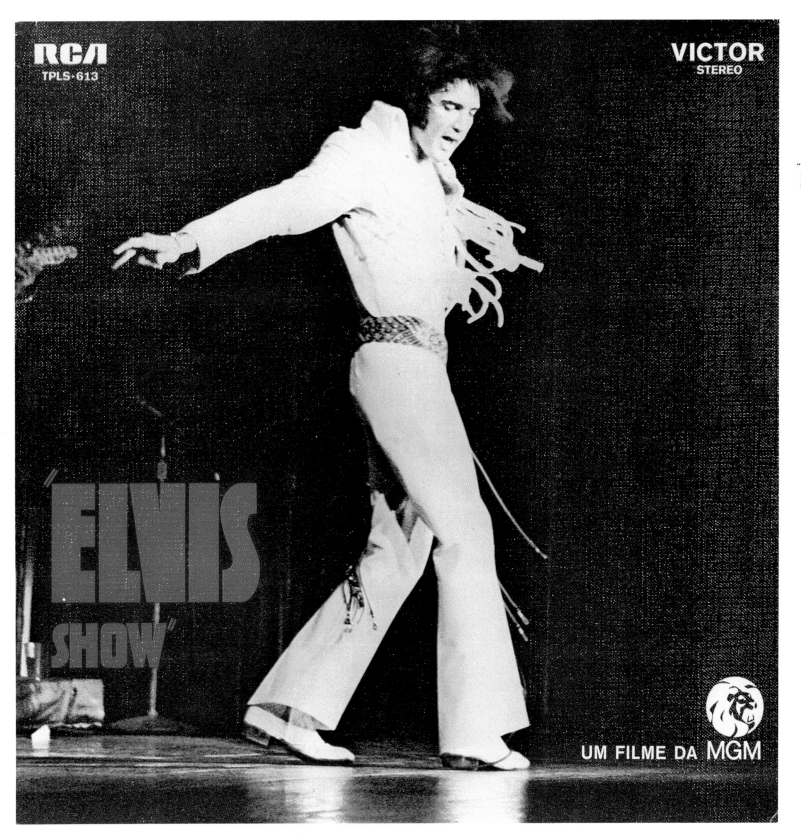

RCA
TPLS-613

VICTOR
STEREO

ELVIS
SHOW"

UM FILME DA MGM

"Elvis Show"
Portùgal (LP)
September 1971

Rags to Riches

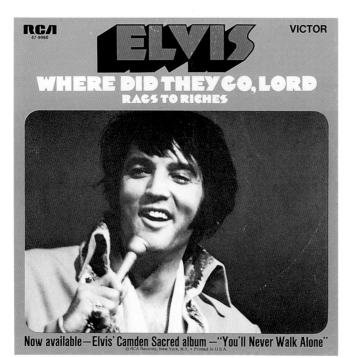

**Where Did They Go, Lord /
Rags to Riches**
United States (single)
February 23, 1971

**Where Did They Go,
Lord / Rags to Riches**
Italy (single)
April 1971

Aloha from Hawaii

Elvis's televised broadcast via satellite from Hawaii in January 1973 was the most watched TV show ever at that time. The LP was distributed a little over a month after the show aired. The first pressings were issued with special "Sneak Preview" stickers, and a limited number were made available to the sponsor, Chicken of the Sea. This sticker was omitted when the commercial version was released. Many photographs from the performance subsequently appeared on single and LP covers.

Aloha from Hawaii
United States (LP)
February 24, 1973

RCA

CAMDEN
CDS 1150

ELVIS
THE U.S. MALE

U.S. MALE / WE'LL BE TOGETHER / ALMOST IN LOVE
IT'S A MATTER OF TIME / LET'S FORGET ABOUT THE STARS
MY LITTLE FRIEND / I'LL TAKE LOVE / BURNING LOVE
IF I'M A FOOL (FOR LOVING YOU)
TODAY, TOMORROW AND FOREVER
LET'S BE FRIENDS / NO MORE

The U.S. Male
England (LP)
June 1975

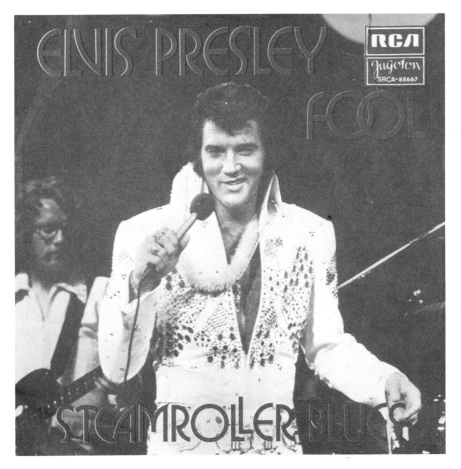

Fool / Steamroller Blues
Yugoslavia (single)
June 1973

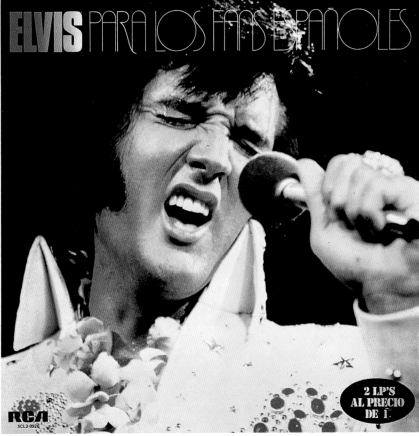

Para los Fans Españoles
Spain (LP)
1976

Separate Ways

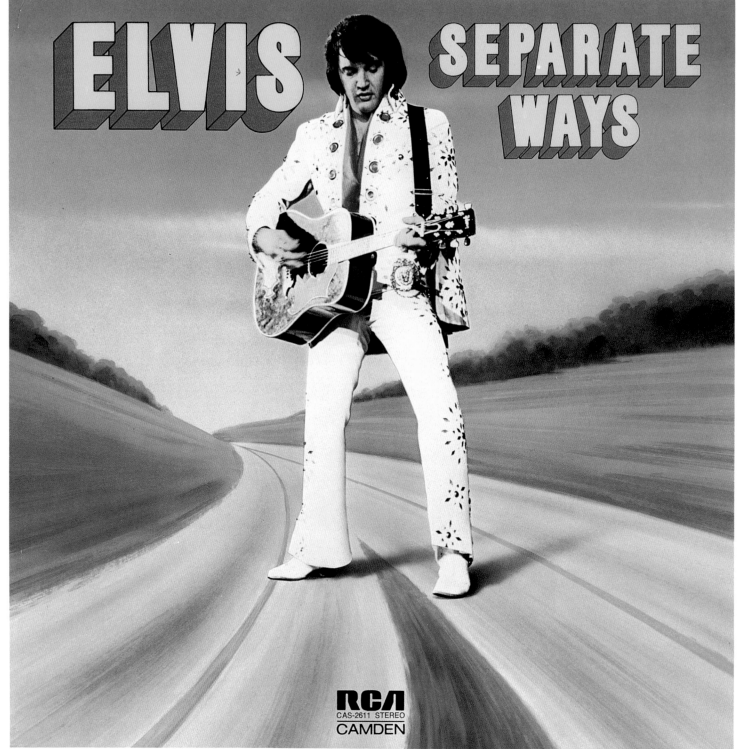

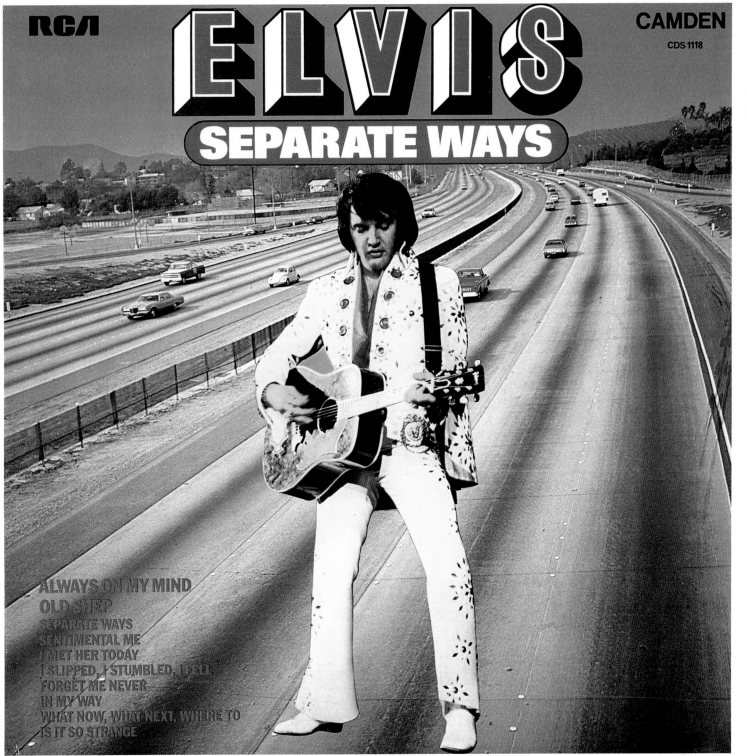

Separate Ways
England (LP)
May 1973

Moody Blue

**Moody Blue /
She Thinks I Still Care**
Portugal (LP)
1977

Moody Blue
United States (single)
June 1977

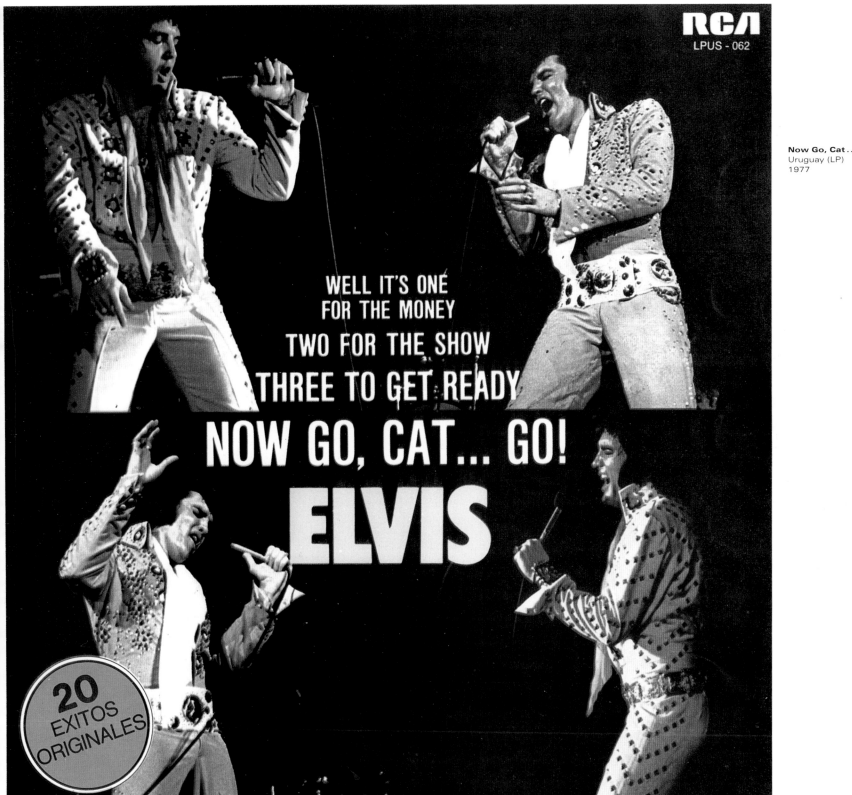

Now Go, Cat...Go!
Uruguay (LP)
1977

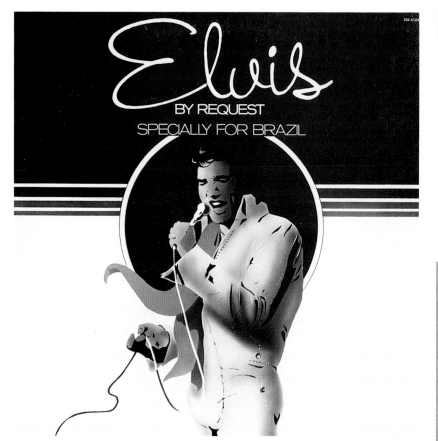

By Request
Specially for Brazil
Brazil (LP)
1979

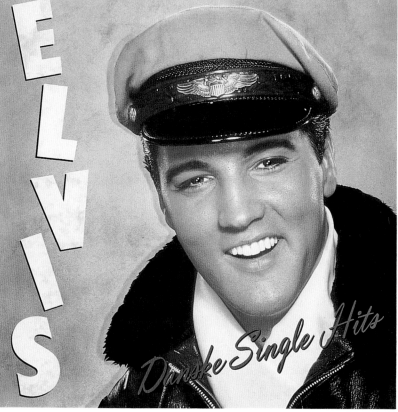

Danske Single Hits
Denmark (LP)
February 1991

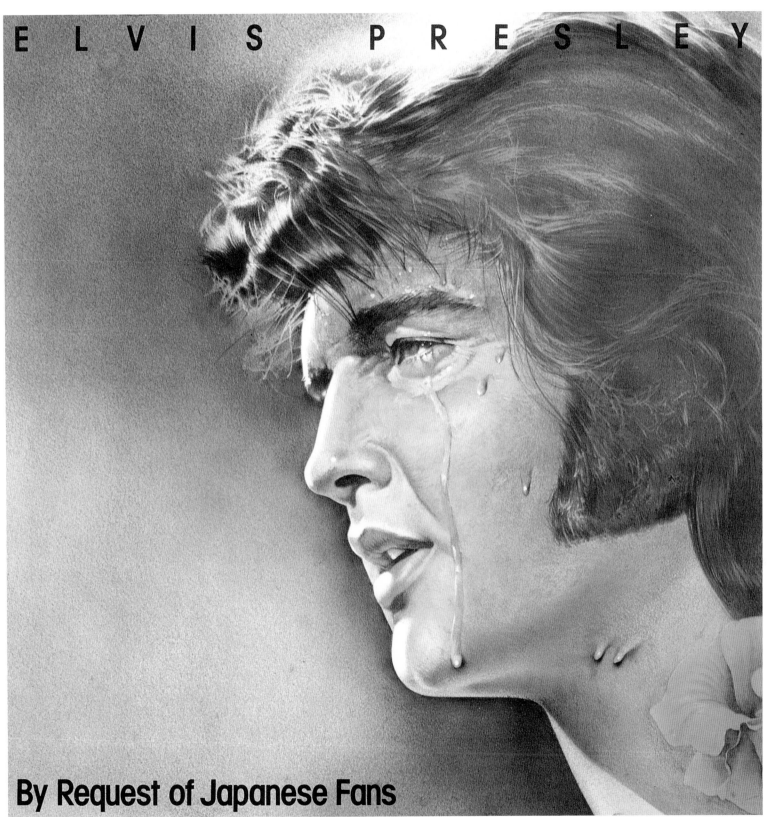

ELVIS PRESLEY

By Request of Japanese Fans

By Request of Japanese Fans
Japan (4-LP box set)
August 1980

Movie Hits

Movie Songs
Finland (LP)
1982

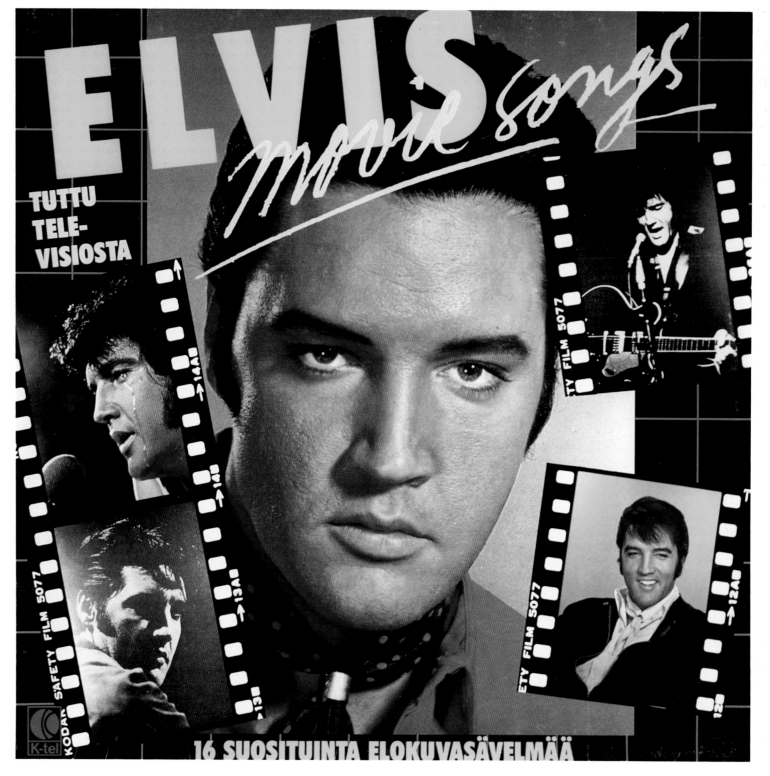

32 Film Hits
Germany (LP)
1984

The Las Vegas Years

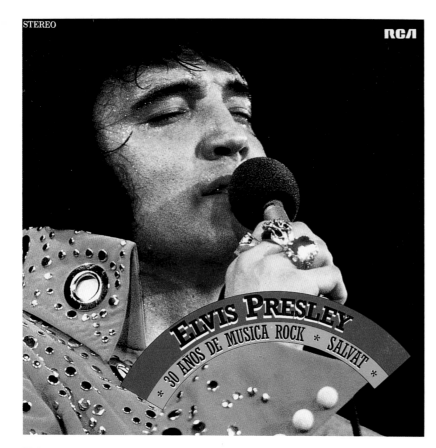

30 Anos de Musica Rock
Mexico (LP)
1984

Lovin' Arms/
You Asked Me To
Bolivia (single)
1980

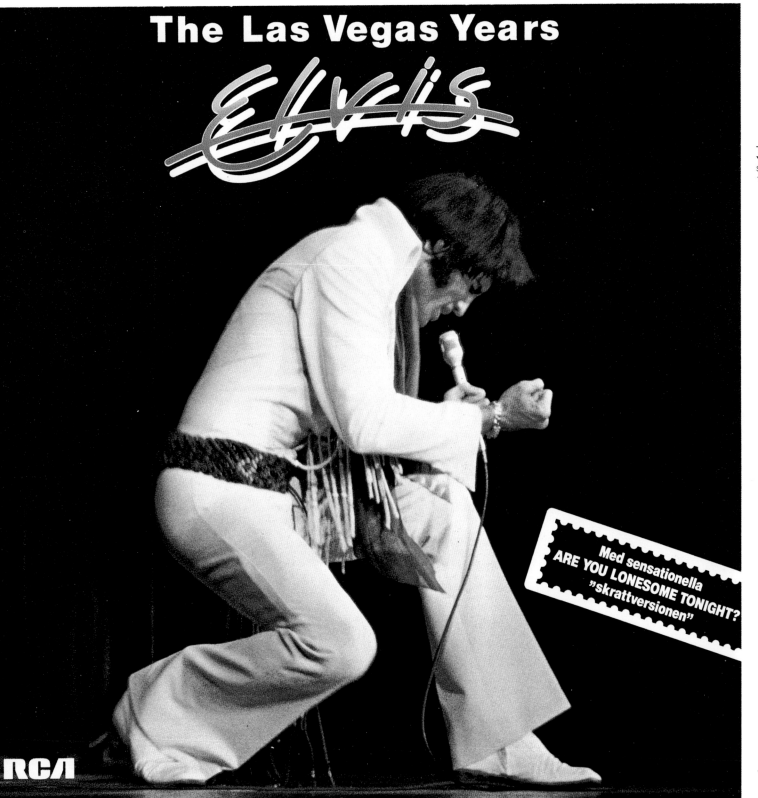

The Las Vegas Years

ELVIS

Med sensationella ARE YOU LONESOME TONIGHT? "skrattversionen"

RCA

The Las Vegas
Years
Sweden (LP)
1980

Elvis Favorites

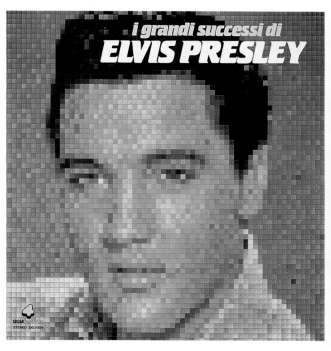

**20 Fantastic Hits
Vol. 2**
Germany (LP)
1981

**I Grandi Successi
di Elvis Presley**
Italy (LP)
1983

ALWAYS ON MY MIND

50TH ANNIVERSARY SPECIAL EXTENDED PLAY EDITION FEATURING:
ALWAYS ON MY MIND • *TOMORROW NIGHT* • *AIN'T THAT LOVIN' YOU BABY* • *DARK MOON*

ELVIS PRESLEY

Always on My Mind
England (12" EP)
July 1985

The Rocker Lives

Rock 'n' Roll Rebel
Ireland (LP)
1982

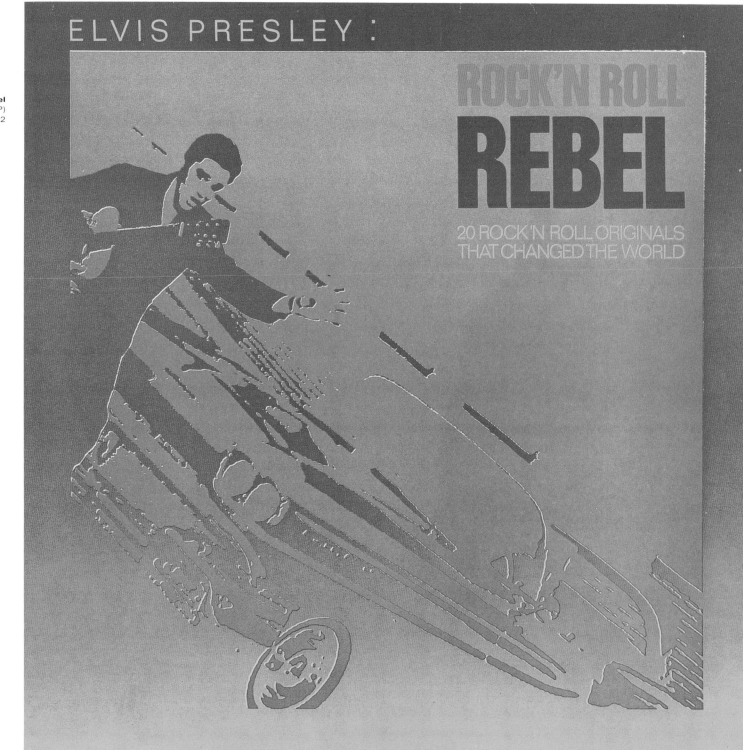

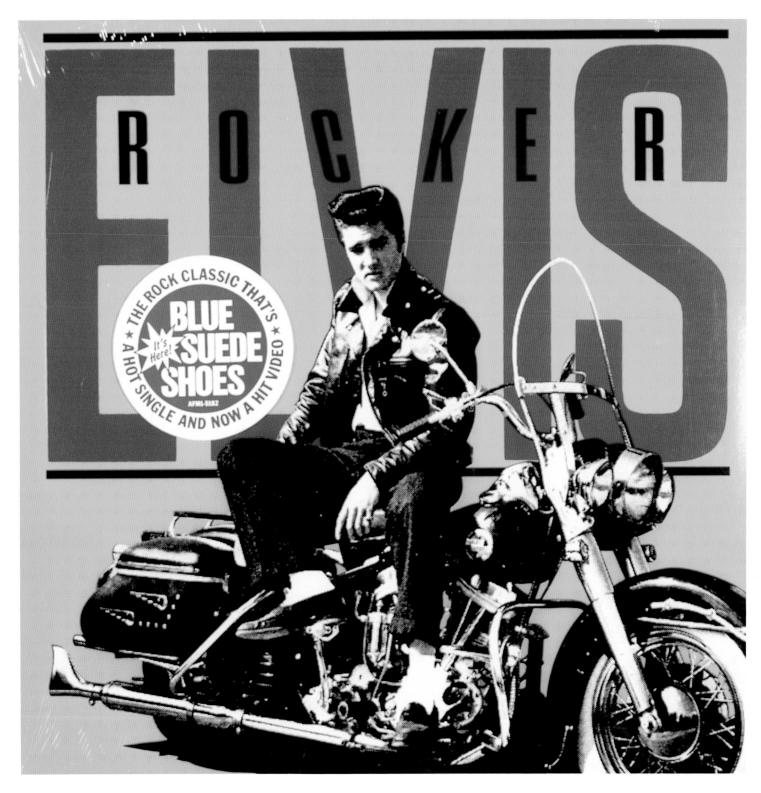

The Rocker
United States (LP)
September 1984

Reconsider Baby
United States (LP)
March 1985

Acknowledgments

There are so many people I wish to thank for helping me in the preparation of this book. This list includes just about everyone who has been a vital part of my life since Elvis Presley entered it.

First and foremost, I would like to thank my mother, who passed away in 1989. Even though she could never understand my "collecting disease," she was always there to help me. Somehow I convinced her to lend me $500 to start a business selling extras of records from my collection. God knows what I would be doing now if it were not for her. Thanks go to her for all her patience and love.

My collection would not be as extensive as it is without the help and knowledge of an early big collector, Peter J. Milne from Aberdeen, Scotland. I would not have known what records existed in other countries without his help. Wherever you are Pete, thanks a million and drop me a line. *You* should have been the one doing this book!

I would not have the collection I do without the following people. Many thanks to the original "team": Carlos Ares and Ariel Llorente Gonzalez (Argentina); Wayne Hawthorne (Australia); Moacyr Jaeger and Norton Coll (Brazil); Carlos Arancibia Castillo and Antonio Alamo (Chile); Ernst Jorgensen (Denmark); Deke Wheeler (England); Jean Marc Gargiulo and Jo Jo Bellanger (France); Gerry Ryff (Holland); Livio Monari (Italy); Haruo Hirose (Japan); and Doug Grant (originally from New Zealand and now living in Australia).

In addition: John Campbell, Wayne Jordan, and Walter Pacheco (Canada); Marcelo Costa (Brazil); Malcolm Rebello, George Cooper, Andrew· Pontoni, and Chris Adams (Australia); Peter Schittler and Peter Baumann (Austria); Etienne Heyndrickx and Willy Suffys (Belgium); Erik Rasmussen (Denmark); Charly Fontaine (France); Helmut Radermacher (Germany); Evaggelos Prious (Greece); Zahir Chinoy (India); Danny Lior (Israel); Bjorn Hellem and Erik Viervoll (Norway); Tito Delgado (Peru); Howard Banney, Maria Columbus, Al Cooley, Lou Fanty, Dale Hampton, Dave Marshall, and Dave Petrelle (United States).

Special thanks to: Jim Curtin, who instructed me in the history of U.S. releases and introduced me to a world I never knew existed ("SPs," "TV GUIDEs," "Dinah Shores," etc.); Sam Theaker for helping me turn a hobby into a business while still keeping the hobby, and for his friendship and honesty; Juan Luis Gonzalez (Dominican Republic) for all the ideas he has given me and for his friendship; and Jimmy Carpenter for all his help and his artistic genius.

I want to particularly thank:

Bruce Marpel (wherever he is now) for introducing me to Elvis Presley. Little did he know what he started!

Wickie Bullock (my first love!) for suffering through all the Elvis movies I took her to back in 1963. Wherever you are today, I still think of you.

Martha Malooly for putting up with my "Elvis addiction" from 1973 to 1976. Thanks for listening to many hours of talking about "Golden Boy," "SPD 23," etc. And special thanks to Martha's mother for all the Sunday dinners and for letting me bring all those characters into her home.

Barbara Barrows, who came into my life after the addiction calmed down. My life wouldn't have been as enjoyable without you.

Sue Horner for always being here for me.

Debbie Trone for sticking by me through some tough times.

Lisa Dowling for being—Lisa!

Brenda Brown for being a really good friend and for understanding me more than most.

Patricia McEnroe for an incredible year! I still miss you, Princess.

Patricia's lovely mother Marie, her sister Ann, her brother Peter, and Dr. Mike.

And last, but not least, the incredibly lovely Laura Loro, probably the most perfect girl in the whole wide world! Thanks for everything you've done for me. I could never have found a nicer person and truer friend.

I also want to thank the following people, without whose help this book would not have been possible: Bob Markel, my agent, who was responsible for bringing this book to Abrams. I could not have found anyone better than Bob, the most knowledgeable and professional person I have met in the book publishing world; Andrew Alef, who worked at BMG and who made me realize that a book such as this one, which I thought about doing years ago, would be of interest to the public; Cal Morgan at St. Martin's Press for all of his help initially; Jerry McConnell for his help in creating the "dummy" that was used to present this book to publishers; Gary Graifman for all his help in obtaining permission from BMG to use the record covers; Toula Ballas, Elisa Urbanelli, and Ellen Nygaard Ford at Abrams for all their help; and Gabe Palacio for taking the great photos used in this book.

The following people at RCA (BMG), New York, deserve thanks: First, my good friend of almost twenty years, Ernst Jorgensen, who asked me to help RCA (BMG) with material for the '50s, '60s, and '70s *Masters* box sets. Because Ernst got me involved with BMG, I met Bernadette Moore (head of the RCA Archives at BMG in New York) who generously opened her files to help me do research for my forthcoming "Elvis Price Guide." Without Bernadette's invitation to visit RCA, I would never have met Vinnie Longo (BMG International), who gave me access to information in the International files. Thanks go to Bruce Hailstalk ("The King of the Vaults") for all the help he gave me in general and for introducing me to the production cards; Jamie Pawliczek and the BMG legal department for their permission to use the covers in this book; Ann Lexmond for her invaluable help at RCA special products; Linda DeMuro for sending me information on RCA/RCA licensees in other countries years ago; and Dick Baxter, Nancy Chesiere, Chick Crumpacker, Hank Hoffman, Tom Krauss, Ed Osborne, Bruce Scavuzzo, Frankie Pezella, and Dan Stopfer.

And I'd like to acknowledge all my other very good friends over the years: Frank Albanese, Linda Appicello, Gail Battisti, Bill "The Judge" Berryman, Pete Campbell, Ray Diebel, Skip Dugdale, Judy Elsner, Marcus Federsel, Craig Flanders, John Flanigan, The Flea, Anita Gold, Elwood Grimm, Elaine Harkins, Sensei Steve Henderson, Beverly and Wally Kahn, The Great Steve La Manna, Maria Myers, Lois Nugent, Don Seigel, Joe Shumard, Jay Smith and Pretty Patty, Steve Smith, Liz Stanne, Lynda and Danny Valetto, Jim Williamson, and The Smooser.

Special thanks to Brian Wilson for all the inspiration, comfort, and enjoyment his music has given me since 1961. I realize that I'm known as an Elvis fanatic, but I never get tired of listening to Brian's songs and his incredible voice.

Last, but not least, I would like to thank posthumously some friends who have recently passed away: John Walhermfechtel, who spent hours every week trying to help me to use my computer. As I type this, it's still hard to believe he's not here. Lyndol Bailey, my pal from Cape May, N.J., whom I miss a lot. Summers won't be the same without his company on the beach. Teddy Wilson, super fantastic pianist from Cape May, who died unexpectedly in 1994. I really miss him. And Gig Williams, another great friend from Cape May, who passed away in 1995.